# LIGHT STRIKE

## HARRIER IIs, HORNETS AND CORSAIR IIs

# LIGHT STRIKE

## HARRIER IIs, HORNETS AND CORSAIR IIs

Joe Cupido and Tony Holmes

First published in Great Britain in 1993
by Osprey, an imprint of
Reed Consumer Books Limited
Michelin House, 81 Fulham Road,
London SW3 6RB
and Auckland, Melbourne, Singapore
and Toronto

ISBN 1 855323095

Edited by Tony Holmes
Page design by Paul Kime
Printed in Hong Kong

**Front cover** This close-up shot focuses on
the area of major difference between the
two versions of the Harrier II; the TAV-8B's
forward fuselage has been stretched by just
under four feet to accommodate the
instructor's cockpit. Fully equipped with all
the offensive avionics of the original AV-
8B, the 'twin-holer' is, however, only
rigged for a single weapons pylon under
each wing; the aircraft usually toting TERs
configured for Mk 76s, LAU-68 rocket
launchers or simply 300-gal external tanks.
As is clearly visible in this shot, the TAV-8B
also lacks the required plumbing for the
scabbed on refuelling probe

**Back cover** VFA-87 'Golden Warriors' were
amongst the last F/A-18A users at Cecil
Field. Not until mid-1991 did the unit pass
on its Lot IX Hornets to reserve-manned
VFAs -204 and -205, receiving Lot XIV
F/A-18Cs in their place. Twelve months
prior to their equipment changeover, the
squadron was heavily involved in CVW-8's
work-up at Naval Air Station (NAS) Fallon,
VFA-87 being called on to perform both
strike and CAP sorties during 17 days of
exhilarating flying over the 'live' ranges.
Carrying only a Cubic Corporation TACTS
(Tactical Air Combat Training System) AIS
(Airborne Instrumentation Sub-system)
data-transmission telemetry pod on its port
stores pylon, this jet rolls out at the head of
a VFA-87 flight tasked with performing an
Alpha Strike CAP against the seasoned
instructors of VFA-127 'Cylons' in their
A-4Fs and F-5Es. The AIS pod monitors
airspeed, angle of attack, attitude, altitude
and simulated weapons, and relays this
information to ground control sites, via
microwave telemetry, in real time. The
complex main gear arrangement settled on
by McAir is well illustrated in this head-on
view, its 'bent knee' construction giving the
aircraft adequate ground stability and wide
undercarriage tracking, without impinging
on the Sparrow missile troughs. To achieve
this, the legs turn through 90 ° as they
retract rearwards for stowage, finishing up
lying flat at the base of the intake ducts
once the gear cycle has been completed.
Fabricated primarily from steel by
Cleveland Pneumatic, the legs are fitted
with Bendix wheels and brakes and
Goodrich tyres, the latter being pressurized
to 350 psi for carrier deck operations. This
figure is halved for shore-based flying

**Title page** Few retired military aircraft get
to enjoy the attention of doting civil
owners, who maintain their weary warriors
in a condition befitting a seasoned combat
veteran. Originally destined to be gutted
and stuffed, and then placed on a pole
alongside the VFA-127- marked A-4 at the
main gate of Naval Air Station (NAS)
Fallon, this once proud A-7B Corsair II now
quietly rots in a corner of the vast base, all
but forgotten by its former masters.
Suffering a serious case of FOD (just look at
all that dirt in its gaping intake), this
aircraft spent its last years with reserve-
manned VA-304 'Firebirds' at NAS
Alameda, in San Francisco. Initially
established on 1 July 1970 and equipped
with A-4Ls, the 'Firebirds' traded up to A-
7Bs later in the decade. The Bravoes were
replaced by definitive Echo models in the
mid-1980s just as the former's chronic
engine problems were reaching the
terminal phase. In 1989 the squadron bade
farewell to the trusty Corsair IIs and
welcomed ex-Marine A-6E Intruders in
their place. After its retirement in 1985,
'Firebird 413' was flown to Davis-Monthan
and temporarily put out to pasture.
Following a request from Fallon's
commanding officer for a second gate
guard, the jet was dusted off and flown on
a one-way sortie north. The base CO was
duly posted after serving his time in
Nevada, and with him went any
enthusiasm for a second gate guard. After
sitting in the Naval Strike Warfare Center
(NSWC) compound covered in tarpaulins
for several years, the jet was eventually
towed into the desert and unceremoniously
dumped on its belly, thus giving the base
fire crews the opportunity to practice their
extraction techniques from time to time.
This is how the airframe looked in January
1992

For a catalogue of all books published by Osprey Aerospace
please write to:

**The Marketing Department, Reed Consumer Books,
1st Floor, Michelin House, 81 Fulham Road, London SW3 6RB**

**Above** As the sun slowly slides below the horizon, the pilot completes his instrument checks and prepares for spool up on the stern of the amphibious assault carrier USS *Belleau Wood* (LHA-3). For two decades the setting of the sun would have marked the end of the day's flying for Marine Corps AV-8 Harrier squadrons, the aircraft's basic navigation and targeting equipment excluding it from nocturnal sorties in all but the most pressing of circumstances. However, the bulge on the nose of this jet denotes that it is configured as an AV-8B(NA) Night Attack Harrier II, the first of the breed fitted with equipment that allows it to function effectively 24 hours a day. Photographed in March 1992 off the California coast, this anonymous silhouette is actually a VMA-211 'Wake Island Avengers' Harrier II, the Marine Corps Air Station (MCAS) Yuma-based unit being the first squadron in the force to convert onto the AV-8B(NA) variant

# Introduction

For many years the term 'light strike' has meant just that, a squadron with this appellation being tasked with supporting the heavy attack units within a carrier air wing (CVW) or Marine air group (MAG). By tradition, a typical aircraft of this genre was a single-seater, blessed with a bomb load that was usually delivered with some precision in the hours of daylight – 'leave the pin-point stuff in bad weather at night to the A-6 jocks' was the official line.

Two of the types featured in this volume fit easily into the above-mentioned definition of a 'light striker'. The A-4 and A-7 were designed to be built and operated in large numbers from the Navy's burgeoning fleet of carriers. Typically the most prolific squadrons within an air wing, the Skyhawk and Corsair II units would provide the 'beef' in the Navy's much vaunted Alpha strike mission package. Similarly, the Marines relied on an impressive 'backbone' of Skyhawk units to enforce their close air support tasking both in war and peace for over three decades. Neither the A-4 or A-7 boasted much in the way of trick avionics, the precision aspect of the aircrafts' ordnance delivery coming primarily from the pilot, who had been trained to get the best out of his equipment.

In the early 1980s the strict delineation between attack and fighter 'pukes' which had existed since the Korean War began to blur as the McDonnell Douglas F/A-18 Hornet started to enter frontline service. Here was an aircraft that could destroy a target with clinical precision and then shoot down any enemy fighters that tried to hinder its passage back to friendly territory. More of an all-rounder than even McAir's legendary F-4 Phantom II, the Hornet revolutionised the light strike community.

At about the same time the Marine Corps was also ushering into service a type which broke with convention; the AV-8B Harrier II. Although in designation the aircraft appeared to be just an uprated follow-on from the AV-8A (a type that had served the Corps well throughout the 1970s), in practice the Harrier II was a weapon built for the 1990s, with growth potential to match. Now serving in large numbers on both coasts, the Harrier II boasts an avionics fit second only to its MAG partner, the F/A-18.

With defence budgets shrinking year after year, and the US Navy being forced to broaden the capabilities of its carrier battle groups, the light strike community is assuming far greater importance within the air wing structure. More F/A-18s are now crowding the decks of carriers on both coasts as AirPac and AirLant replace the strictly one role Tomcat and Intruder squadrons with multi-role Hornet-equipped units. And these aircraft are not even coming from the traditional light strike strongholds at Lemoore and Cecil Field. They are wearing 'Marine' titling and hail from El Toro and Beaufort!

The next generation F/A-18E/F programme is currently viewed by the Pentagon as the backbone around which the CVW of the year 2000 will be built, and congress has duly respected the Navy's wishes by maintaining the funding for the aircraft at a workable level. Similarly, proposals for the Harrier II's eventual replacement have also recently been called for, and this programme is another that should find funds a little easier to come by than most.

As a result of their willingness to adapt to and perform virtually any task thrust upon them over the past 35 years, the respective light strike communities of the Navy and Marines are currently in the healthiest position in terms of numbers, operational capability and funding of any group in their branch of the armed forces.

**Right** Prior to receiving Harrier IIs, VMA-211 had enjoyed a long-term relationship with the A-4 Skyhawk – 32 years and 6 months to be exact! In that time they operated five different models of the 'Bantam Bomber', the last version to feature on the squadron ramp being the A-4M. Following their replacement, the Skyhawks flew west to NAS Alameda and the reserve-manned VMA-133 'Golden Gators'. This distinctive silhouette was captured during the return transit to the aircraft's San Francisco base following a successful strike sortie on the Chocolate Mountain Military Operating Area in December 1991

# Contents

# 'Bantam Bomber'

**Right** The diminutive A-4 performed much of the US Navy's 'bomb truckin'' work over both North and South Vietnam for the first six years of the war in South-east Asia. This dangerous mission tasking resulting in the loss of 195 Skyhawks in combat between 1964 and 1973, and a further 77 in operational accidents during the same period. Responsible for performing more strike sorties during *Rolling Thunder* than any other naval type, the A-4 also suffered the worst loss rate of any fleet combat aircraft; the Skyhawks downed during the Vietnam conflict represent more than 31 per cent of all aircraft/helicopters lost by the Navy in combat. Of those 195 jets shot down, only one was 'bagged' by the North Vietnamese Air Force (NVAF), this somewhat dubious distinction befalling Lt C D Stackhouse of VA-76 'Spirits' on 25 April 1967 during an Alpha strike south of Hanoi. The lieutenant's A-4C (BuNo 147799) was hit by 23 mm cannon fire from a MiG-17, and following his successful ejection Stackhouse was captured and interned in the infamous 'Hanoi Hilton'— his shooting down was VA-76's first loss of the deployment as part of CVW-21 aboard USS *Bon Homme Richard* (CVA-31). The unit's morale received a serious shot in the arm six days later, however, when Lt Cdr Theodore R Swartz evened up the score during an air wing strike on Kep airfield, situated on the outskirts of Hanoi. Whilst attacking two MiGs on the runway with LAU-10/A 5-in Zuni rockets, mounted in pods beneath the aircraft's wing, Swartz was warned of a pair of MiG-17s in his 'six o'clock' (rear) position. 'I spotted the attacking aircraft and put my A-4 into a high barrel roll, dropping in behind the MiGs. From this markedly advantageous position, I fired several air-to-ground rockets at the Number Two MiG and then got another call that there was a MiG at my 'six o'clock' again. I was not able to see my rockets hit as I bent my A-4 hard, checking for the suspected third MiG', he recalled upon recovering aboard the carrier. Swartz's wingman had, however, seen the MiG-17 bury itself in the ground, and this was more than enough to earn the pilot the only confirmed NVAF A-4 victory of the war. Swartz's kill was one of nine MiG-17s claimed by CVW-21 during the carrier's 112 days on the line in the Tonkin Gulf. The flipside to this impressive tally was that the airwing lost 21 aircraft and six pilots killed or MIA, including a further three VA-76 jets. This pristine A-4C was bought as a surplus airframe from Davis-Monthan by Jim Robinson of Houston, Texas, 20 years after the MiG kill sortie was flown, and painstakingly restored to its former glory in the late 1980s. Fully airworthy, the appropriately marked Skyhawk was recently donated by its owner to the Experimental Aircraft Association (EAA) at Oshkosh, where it operates as part of the Combat Jets Flying Museum fleet

**Above** A total of 160 A-4Ms were built for the Marines in the mid-1970s, the Mikes seeing service with almost a dozen frontline and reserve units prior to the type's final retirement in 1993. No new airframes were delivered to the Navy, however, the Corsair II and then the F/A-18 fulfilling the fleet's strike requirements. How, then, did this airframe (BuNo 158180) become adorned with 'NAVY' titling? At the end of the 1980s the reserve command highlighted the need for a more potent adversary training platform to replace its ageing TA-4Js at the Naval Air Reserve Unit (NARU) at NAS Dallas, Texas. To fill this requirement, they took charge of a dozen A-4Ms fresh from USMC service and sent them to a Naval Air Rework Facility (NARF) where they were stripped of their 20 mm cannon, various internal weapons guidance equipment and wing hardpoints, and configured for adversary work. Most certainly not dressed for the ball, this 'ex-leatherneck' was photographed undergoing its weight loss programme in December 1991

**Left** Of all the myriad Skyhawk models to leave the Douglas plant at El Segundo, California, it is rather ironic that the most populous and long-lived version in the US Navy today is the non-combatant TA-4. Over 150 'two-holers' still ply their trade with no less than 16 frontline and reserve squadrons in 1993, the TA-4Js performing a variety of tasks ranging from basic pilot training at 'nugget' level in Texas and Missouri, to advanced air combat training at Miramar, Oceana and Key West. Falling into the latter category, this tactically camouflaged TA-4J of VC-13 (redesignated VFC-13 in 1988) was photographed on finals to Miramar in March 1985. One of two reserve-manned fighter composite squadrons in the Navy, the 'Saints' traditionally fly more than 50 per cent of their adversary sorties out of 'Fightertown' annually, the full-time-reservists often travelling away from home to various naval air stations along the West Coast to perform roving ACM training. Aside from three of four TA-4Js retained on strength to simulate first generation aircraft in the ACM syllabus, VFC-13 operate around a dozen A-4F 'Super Fox' airframes in the second and third generation slots

**Above** Unencumbered by 'draggy' items like bomb pylons, external tanks or even the 20 'mike-mike' cannon barrels protruding from the wing roots, a 'clean' A-4M in the hands of a highly proficient Texas 'Ranger' can be more than a match for a Tomcat or Hornet – just ask the aircrew at VF-201, -202 or VMFA-112. Being the ultimate Skyhawk in the large A-4 family, it was only fitting that McAir technicians should shoehorn the most powerful version of the venerable Pratt & Whitney J52 engine into the Mike; the J52-P-408 is good for 11,200 lbs of dry thrust when the pilot feels the need to flex the aircraft's muscles. The original A4D-1 (redesignated A-4A in 1962) entered service equippped with the 7800 lb thrust Curtiss-Wright J65-W-4 engine! Tasked almost exclusively with providing ACM training for the Dallas-based Navy and Marine units at Hensley Field, the 'Rangers' have so far refrained from embellishing their Skyhawks with the gaudy camouflage schemes made famous by their full-time brethren at Miramar, Oceana and Key West. Only the red star on the tail and the two digit 'bort' modex on the nose denote that this aircraft has changed roles – woe betide any fighter jock who strays across this 'vanilla' A-4M and thinks that he is fighting a 'jar head'

**Right** Making an early start on the final leg of his cross-country from the NADEP (Naval Aviation Depot) at MCAS Cherry Point, North Carolina, to home plate at Yuma, a lone A-4M 'driver' from VMAT-102 'Hawks' performs an impromptu flyby of the Hill AFB runway as a 'thank you' to the snow plow operator who had to carve the black top out from underneath the snow at the Utah base to allow the jet to depart

**Above** The A-4M entered Marine service just as frontline squadrons were enjoying their most colourful spell in terms of unit markings post-Vietnam. To illustrate the point, here is a typical Mike of the period enjoying a short break on the transient ramp at Hill AFB in February 1976. This airframe was virtually brand new when it was photographed, its pilot having left to fill in some departure forms following his overnight stay in the base BOQ. To avoid having to waddle in his G-suit to and from the 'line shack', he has wisely chosen to hang his 'greens' on the trusty muzzle of the port Mk 12 20 mm cannon. Judging by the sooty deposits around this weapon, the pilot has been indulging in a spot of target strafing during his stay in Utah

**Below** Just as the Mikes enjoyed the highs of full squadron colours, they also had to endure the virtual anonymity of the Tactical Paint Scheme (TPS), which was gradually adopted with some reluctance by the various MAGs in the early 1980s. Photographed departing Hill AFB in April 1982 carrying centreline tanks and empty multiple ejector racks (MER) for Mk 76 25 lb 'blue bombs', these A-4Ms from VMAT-102 'Hawks' clearly show the state of flux existing in many squadrons at the time in regards to individual aircraft colour schemes. The second Mike in the formation wears a 'half-way house' rendition of the squadron's blood red tail fin, as featured on the A-4M in the previous photograph, along with full colour national markings and warning stencils. The leader, on the other hand, has the definitive spec three-shade TPS camouflage as set down by the CNO (Chief of Naval Operations), VMAT-102's only deviation from the norm being the single digit nose and fin tip modexs in white. The squadron provided both type conversion and refresher training primarily for MAG-13's three frontline A-4M units for almost two decades. Reservists, as well as aircrew destined for the Forward Air Controlling (FAC) world of the various Headquarters and Maintenance Squadrons (H&MS), were also channelled through the training syllabus. Operating a large fleet of A-4Ms and TA-4Fs, the unit flew an average of 400 sorties per month and trained 30 to 40 replacement and refresher pilots a year. The curriculum included low altitude tactics, basic air combat manoeuvring and air-to-ground and close air support mission profiles

**Left** As mentioned earlier, the history of this particular squadron and the Skyhawk are inextricably linked over three decades, VMA-211 receiving its first A4D-2s as replacements for their AD-4B Skyraiders on 9 September 1957 at Naval Auxillary Air Station Edenton, North Carolina. Some 32 years and six months later on 21 February 1990 the last A-4M left Yuma bound for VMA-133 at Alameda, thus marking the end of one of the longest squadron/marque partnerships in aviation history. Eight months prior to the unit's phasing out of the Mike, they headed north in force to Klamath Falls Air National Guard Base in Oregon for a large *Lobo Flag* exercise. Operating as enemy aggressor aircraft against the ANG's F-4s, F-15s and F-16s, the 'Avengers' utlized finless AIM-9 captive rounds fitted with standard seeker heads to enhance the value of the training for both attackers and defenders; these are visible on the outer wing pylons of all four jets. Providing ACM training for ANG assets was in complete contrast to their previous mission tasking – the unit had just returned to Yuma after completing their last A-4 deployment to MCAS Iwakuni, Japan. VMA-211 had established strong links with the Japanese air station during its years with the Skyhawk, the 'Avengers' being first based there as far back as late 1958. During the Southeast Asian conflict, VMA-211 used Iwakuni as a permanent base from which to deploy on combat tours into South Vietnam, the squadron making four such dets whilst equipped with A-4Es during an eight-year period from 1965 to 1973, losing 15 aircraft and 7 pilots due to enemy action whilst in-theatre. Returning to MCAS El Toro, California, in August 1976, VMA-211 soon exchanged their veteran Echoes for fresh Mikes. Further Iwakuni dets were made in 1979/80, 1983/84 and 1987, before their final rotation in December 1988

**Above** Wearing a common variation on the TPS scheme seen on many A-4Ms in the early 1980s, this almost anonymous Skyhawk clearly shows the two most prominent shades of grey then in use through the utilization of a mid-fuselage demarcation line. On strength with VMA-311 'Tomcats' when photographed at Yuma in September 1981, the aircraft lacks the unit's familiar 'WL' tail code and flamboyant feline decoration, which suggests that it may have been acquired from another MAG-13 squadron. The significance of the red box containing the word 'SCARFACE' beneath the cockpit is unfortunately lost to posterity – perhaps the aircraft was 'zapped' by a marauding groundcrew from the AH-1 Cobra-equipped HMLA-367 'Scarface' whilst transitting through MCAS Camp Pendleton in California at some stage? Now equipped with AV-8Bs, the 'Tomcats' flew four different variants of the A-4 between 1958 and 1988, and like VMA-211, they spent many years on det at Iwakuni, including a continuous period of eight years during the Vietnam War

**Below** From famine to feast! Wearing what can only be described as a 'Sierra Hotel' scheme, an 18-month-old A-4M of VMA-331 'Bumblebees' makes a no nonsense recovery at Hill AFB during a cross-country from Yuma to Cherry Point in August 1980. A further splash of technicolour is added by interior shading of the split trailing-edge spoilers and starboard airbrake, all of which 'dirty up' the airflow over the aircraft's diminutive wing and help slow the 'pocket rocket' after touchdown. The 'Bumblebees' enjoyed only a relatively brief working relationship with the A-4M as the Cherry Point-based squadron was earmarked to be the first unit to transition onto the AV-8B within the Corps, a task it duly carried out in 1984. Returning to the Skyhawk, VMA-331 also achieved the distinction of receiving the last new-build A-4 to leave the El Segundo factory after almost 25 years of production – airframe number 2960 (BuNo 160264) was delivered to the squadron on 27 February 1979. Equipped progressively with the A-4B, E and finally M from 1959 onwards, the 'Bumblebees' earnt a reputation for lavish decoration of their Skyhawks, the culmination of which was this stunning scheme – even the tailhook and pilot's bonedome conform to squadron colours! Due to ever tightening defence budgets, VMA-331 was one of several Marine frontline fast jet squadrons deactivated in 1992

**Above** Devoid of external stores, bar a pair of 330 gal ferry tanks, a scruffy Mike approaches the trailing drogue (out of shot), deployed from the starboard refuelling pod of a VMGR-152 KC-130R. Probably rather happy to see the lumbering bulk of the MCAS Futenma, Okinawa, based Hercules way out in the middle of the Pacific, the pilot of the unmarked 'Scooter' peers through his Ray-Bans in an effort to line his thirsty A-4 up with the drogue basket. Skyhawks were regular customers for the Marines KC-130 fleet during the aircraft's 30+ years of service, its 'long legs' being stretched to the max by a transpac. The det push was usually conducted in stages via Wake Island or more often Hawaii (Kaneohe Bay), but in a time of crisis a non-stop crossing using both Marine and USAF tanker support and a C-9B Skytrain II from the Navy as a 'mothership' could be made. Most definitely not part of a MAG 'surge', this A-4 was photographed on 22 September 1987 returning to California for a major maintenance overhaul at the NAS North Island NARF following a spell on det with VMA-211. As is standard practice when heading for a long period of non-flying, the aircraft has had its squadron markings removed; note the patches of light TPS grey applied over the nose modex

**Above** Recipients of many of the surplus A-4Ms released by the widespread proliferation of AV-8Bs at Yuma and Cherry Point in the mid to late 1980s were the handful of Marine Reserve Attack squadrons within the 4th Marine Air Wing. Spread across the USA, VMAs -124, -131, -133, -142 and -322 operated a mixed fleet of Vietnam era A-4Es and Fs for almost two decades until the 'next generation' A-4Ms appeared in the mid-1980s. One of those units to benefit from the upgrade in equipment was VMA-133 'Golden Gators' of MAG-46. Photographed rolling out from the squadron pan towards the NAS Alameda runway in December 1991, this veteran was one of several A-4Ms put up by the unit to drop live ordnance on the Chocolate Mountain range within the Twenty Nine Palms military operating area. Befitting an ageing warrior, this A-4M has been loaded up with two 500 lb Mk 82R Snakeye bombs as used in South-east Asia. The Snakeye's pop-out fins are being progressively replaced by the new Goodyear Aerospace BSU-45 air inflatable retard (AIR) bolt on tail, which straps onto the bomb like the former device and improves delivery accuracy. These particular weapons are fitted with more modern BSU-86 fins (a modified and upgraded tail unit). Placing little strain on the 'agricultural looking' centreline TER are six Mk 76 'blue bombs', which simulate the ballistics of the full size Mk 82SEs at a fraction of the latter's cost

**Above** When the first A4Ds entered Marine service in the late 1950s, the clean exterior of the aircraft was one of its more admirable features. Clean flowing lines from stem to stern made the diminutive bomber a handsome sight to behold. Thirty years later, the A-4M appeared to be suffering from a bad case of acne, particularly around the nose of the aircraft. Taking on the appearance of a mod fit designed by a joint services committee, the 'nasal region' of the Mike was festooned with a variety of electronic counter measure (ECM) and weapon delivery aids, the most prominant of which was the Hughes ASB-19(V)-2 Angle Rate Bombing System (ARBS). Designed to provide pin-point targeting information for both laser-guided and conventional bomb delivery, the ARBS utilizes a combined laser and television camera which computes the range and slant angle of the aircraft to the target, relaying this information to the pilot's Head-Up Display (HUD). The remaining excrescenes flanking the laser equipment deal with recording and combating electronic warfare threats encountered by the aircraft in the forward hemishpere; the rear of the aircraft is protected by a similar array of antennae scabbed onto the fin tip and tailpipe fairing. The final protrusion to the left of the ARBS is of course the fixed in-flight refuelling probe

**Left** Systems functioning and the J52 whining away, the pilot has taxied his A-4M to the hammerhead at the threshold of the Alameda runway. Following one last check of the flying surfaces, and a quick engine test at full military power, he will position himself on the black top, push open the throttles, release the brake and commence his bombing sortie. Like the Skyhawk featured in the previous photograph, this A-4 is equipped with a TER load of Mk 76s and two full size Mk 82s, although the standard conical fins on both weapons suggest that these are low-drag general-purpose (LDGP) bombs as opposed to retarded Snakeyes

**Above** Cruising down the California coast at 27,000 ft, this 'Golden Gator' carries a mixed warload of four Mk 82 LDGPs on the centreline TER, and a LAU-10/A four-tube Zuni rocket launcher on each outer wing pylon. The five-inch unguided rockets can be used either as weapons in their own right, or as target markers for other strike aircraft, the latter option being extensively taken up by FAC aircraft (F/A-18D and OV-10) in *Desert Storm*. The staining on the overwing walkway and around the cockpit and tail could be found on all but the most freshly of overhauled A-4Ms camouflage in TPS greys, the porosity of the matt paint used in the application of the low-viz scheme absorbing the everyday flightline grime trodden onto the aircraft during ramp maintenance and aircrew arrival or departure

**Left** Staying well above the theoretical shoulder-launched SAM umbrella, the Marine reserve pilot pickles his 500 lb 'slicks' whilst performing a 20° dive angle delivery run on the vast Chocolate Mountain range. The whispy tufts of smoke beneath the jet are the remnants of a Zuni marker flare fired at the briefed target by another VMA-133 A-4M. With total air superiority assured during the 1991 Gulf War, Marine and Navy light stike assets were free to attack targets in much of Kuwait and Iraq from this relatively safe altitude

**Above and right** First runs successfully completed, two of the Skyhawks form up to clear the area prior to ingressing from another direction so as to maximize the training benefit derived from expending live ordnance on simulated targets. The Skyhawk's modest physical appearance can be gauged from the seemingly oversized external tanks bolted beneath the wings of both aircraft. The fairing immediately aft of the tailhook contains the brake parachute. Judging by the decoration of the wingman's bonedome, this particular 'leatherneck' was hoping to receive F/A-18 Hornets in place of the venerable Skyhawks sometime in the near future – budget cuts unfortunately put paid to his multirole machinations, VMA-133 being deactivated on 30 September 1992

**Above** Beetling back up the rugged coastline over an oily smooth Pacific Ocean, the pilot of A-4M BuNo 158173 banks his jet towards the evening sun, thus perfectly illuminating the aircraft for photography. Built as part of the first batch of 49 Mike models delivered in the early 1970s, this airframe served with various frontline attack squadrons before ending up at Alameda in late 1990. The A-4M production line was open for no less that nine years, although the end figure of 158 brand new airframes built in that time clearly indicates that McAir were concentrating on the construction of other frontline types. By the beginning of 1993, this sight was a rarity in American skies, with only a handful of A-4Ms still being operated by reserve-manned VMA-124 'Whistling Death' at NAS Memphis, Tennessee, and VMA-131 'Diamondbacks' at NAS Willow Grove, Philadelphia, as this volume went to press. In a deal struck soon after a flood of A-4Ms began arriving at the storage facility at Davis-Monthas AFB in the second half of 1992, the US State Department agreed to sell 54 Skyhawks to the Argentine Navy for virtually immediate delivery

**Right** Naval aircraft have traditionally been designed with ease of maintenance and the cramped confines of a hangar deck firmly in mind. Because of these criteria, the A-4 was built in such a way so as to allow it to be broken down into component parts in a matter of hours without the use of any special jigs. Bereft of its tail unit, this veteran Skyhawk was in the process of receiving 'open J52 surgery' when it was photographed in VMA-133's hangar at Alameda in December 1991. As is plainly obvious from this anatomical view, the Skyhawk's fuselage circumference is barely large enough to house the Pratt & Whitney turbojet and its associated plumbing – hence the need for an external hump on the later model A-4s when the Navy and Marines specified more sophisticated avionics. Still on the topic of the aircraft's internal space, the recent upgrading of the Royal New Zealand Air Force's A-4Ks through the *Project Kahu* refit has seen the hump dispensed with once and for all, the miniaturization of the upgraded avionics allowing the new equipment to be fitted in the nose of the Skyhawk

**Above** Prior to receiving Mikes in late 1989, VMA-133 had fulfilled its duties with MAG-46 for over a decade equipped with firstly Echoes and then Foxtrot model Skyhawks. Most of the reserve squadrons initially experienced serious serviceability problems with their 'new' mounts following their delivery, the level of 'electrickery' associated with the A-4M far outweighing that embodied in the austere A-4F. The supply of spare parts and a general lack of hands-on experience with the ARBS and relatively sophisticated ECM suite were targeted as the main problem areas, but as is always the case with the reserve, the units knuckled down to the task at hand, and by the time the Mikes were retired to Arizona in 1992/93, the groundcrews were achieving higher availability rates with the aircraft than when they were in frontline service! The lack of uniformity in the varying shades of grey used even at this late stage in the aircraft's career are worthy of note, the darker shade used to pick out the detail markings on BuNo 159779 contrasting with the pale grey employed on BuNo 158160 (the 'Boss Bird')

**Right** The 20 'Mike Mike' would be hard pressed to inflict the same amount of damage on a target as an M61A1 Gatling gun, but it would force soldiers on the ground to seek shelter rather than engage the strafing A-4 driver with small arms fire. Simply a revolver that has been refined from a World War 2 Hispano cannon design, the gas-operated Mk 12 Colts were each fed by wing-mounted magazines which contained 200 rounds per gun. A compact weapon of modest size, the gun's ease of maintenance and light weight made it popular with squadron armourers

**Above** Bathed in gloriously warm summer sunshine, a pristine TA-4F of
Headquarters and Maintenance Squadron (H&MS) 32 rolls along the taxy
track as a pair of veteran RF-8G Crusaders from VFP-63 climb away from the
runway in full afterburner. Photographed in August 1979, this 'vanilla'
Skyhawk was at the time just beginning to share ramp space back at Cherry
Point with a handful of seriously militarized 'two-holers' that had been
reconfigured as 'fastFAC' OA-4Ms. In fact, the airframes built on either side
of this Skyhawk at El Segundo were sent to the NARF at Pensacola and
modified accordingly, before returning to H&MS-32. Prior to assuming the
FAC role, this unit had mainly performed communication and liaison tasks
between the various air stations within Fleet Marine Force Atlantic, although
an earlier generation of H&MS pilots had flown FAC missions for real in
plain TA-4Fs over Vietnam in the late 1960s

**Below** Wearing the appropriate warpaint, a pukka OA-4M of Marine Air Logistics Squadron (MALS) 11 'Outlaws' passes through Hill AFB on a snowy modification delivery flight from Pensacola to El Toro. Whilst in the hands of the NARF at the idyllic Florida air station, the formerly austere TA-4F was gutted internally and reconfigured with the following equipment: ARC-159 UHF air comms radio; VHF radio for ground communications; ARN-118 TACAN; KY-28 secure voice system; ALQ-126 electronic counter-measures equipment; and an ARL-45/50 radar warning system. An A-4M-style dorsal hump was added to house much of this kit, whilst the various nose and tail excrescences associated with the ECM and RWR kit duly appeared. The sophisticated (for an A-4 at least!) comms fit shoehorned into the aircraft allowed the two-man FAC team to instantly relay co-ordinates to both air and ground forces. When passing on the position of a target the pilot could choose to mark it with his own Zuni smoke rockets, or task other aircraft or artillery/naval gunfire/mortars to perform this crucial job. Only 23 OA-4Ms were remanufactured from October 1978, this small number of airframes being split between units on both coasts of America. As with many of the A-4Ms, the 'fastFACs' were retired from service in 1990, MAGs -12 and -32 sending their surviving 14 airframes to various destinations from their Iwakuni and Cherry Point homes: one was placed on permanent display within Iwakuni air station itself; two went to Davis-Monthan for storage; one was passed to the NADEP at Cherry Point; and the remaining ten have been taken on charge by the Naval Air Test Center (NATC) at NAS Patuxent River, Maryland, as chase-plane replacements for a similar number of TA-7Cs that were recently retired

# 'SLUF'

**Right** The versatile and seemingly ageless A-4 was replaced by the similarly rugged LTV A-7 Corsair II at the Navy's two large light strike facilities at Lemoore, California, and Cecil Field, Florida. Over a period of six years from 1967 to 1973, no less than 29 squadrons converted onto the Corsair II, several of these units having retired their venerable A-1 Skyraiders in favour of the 'SLUF'. Like all other Navy aircraft of the period, the A-7 was liberally decorated in garish squadron colours, a tradition many units carried over from their Skyhawk or Skyraider days. Photographed at Lemoore in May 1979, this suitably decorative A-7E proudly wears the colours of VA-22 'Fighting Redcocks' in strategic locations all over its fuselage. Ten years earlier, similarly marked A-4Fs were heavily involved in strike missions flown over South Vietnam and Laos from the USS *Bon Homme Richard* (CVA-31), this particular cruise being the fourth in a series of five deployments made by VA-22 between 1965 and 1970 whilst equipped with the Skyhawk. Carrying a less war-like load on this occasion, the Corsair II is equipped with a standard Navy-issue D-704 refuelling pod beneath the port wing and a pair of appropriately marked 250 gal tanks to starboard to balance the aircraft up. Veteran light strike naval aviators often remarked that this particular configuration was their least favourite for the A-7 as the aircraft's less than gutsy powerplant only just allowed them to recover from a 'bolter' on a carrier deck when hamstrung with three tanks. A closer inspection of this aircraft reveals that it has recently had its port windscreen panel replaced, perhaps due to a birdstrike

**Opposite** Upon the squadron's return to Lemoore in December 1970 following its fifth and last Skyhawk WestPac, VA-22 quickly transitioned onto the A-7E with the help of VA-122, the Pacific Fleet Replacement Air Group (RAG) unit. After a brief work-up period with the jet, VA-22 was assigned to CVW-15 (along with sister-squadron VA-94 'Mighty Shrikes') and despatched to the war zone once again. On station aboard USS *Coral Sea* (CV-43) from 12 November 1971 to 17 July 1972, the 'Fighting Redcocks' were heavily involved in *Blue Tree*, *Freedom Train* and *Linebacker* operations throughout the cruise. Three A-7s were lost during this period – two to SAMs and one to unknown causes – and unfortunately only one pilot was recovered from the downed aircraft. A fourth jet was lost in a non-fatal accident during routine operations. On 9 March 1973 the squadron headed west again, but this time the newly signed Paris Peace Accords had taken effect and VA-22's operational sorties were restricted to missions over Laos and Cambodia. No losses were recorded and the unit returned to Lemoore in November. Over the next 17 years the 'Fighting Redcocks' performed a series of WestPac cruises, participating in countless exercises and air wing work-ups at Fallon and El Centro. From 1982 the squadron's at sea home was USS *Enterprise* (CVN-65), VA-22 finally bidding farewell to the *'Big E'* at the end of the carrier's final pre-refit around-the-world cruise in March 1990. That same year the unit also retired its Corsair IIs to Davis-Monthan, thus ending a 20-year association with the pugnacious Vought jet. The 'SLUF' was replaced by the F/A-18C, this aircraft bringing with it a change in designation to VFA-22 to better reflect their increased capability. Still assigned to CVW-11, the 'Fighting Redcocks' now ply their trade from the steel decks of the *Nimitz* class carrier USS *Abraham Lincoln* (CVN-72). Looking back to when this photograph was taken in May 1979, VA-22 was busy readying itself for an extended WestPac with CVW-15 aboard USS *Kitty Hawk* (CV-63), which commenced at the end of the month and was not completed until February of the following year due to the revolution in Iran. 'Redcock 302' was flown throughout the cruise by squadron XO, Cdr Jerry Palmer

**Left** Of the trio of Skyraider squadrons that transitioned onto the Corsair II in the late 1960s only this particular outfit – VA-25 'First of the Fleet' – are still in the light strike business today. Now equippped with the very latest Lot 14 night attack F/A-18Cs currently in service, VA-25's standard equipment looked like this 15 years ago. Captured on Kodachrome 64 whilst passing through Hill AFB in May 1978, A-7E BuNo 159266 wears a decidedly unsubtle unit marking on its tail, as well as the distinctive 'NE' tail codes of CVW-2. Although assigned to USS *Ranger* (CV-61) at the time, the squadron spent much of the year ashore at Lemoore performing routine exercises and work-ups. In fact, VA-25 did not deploy to sea until February of the following year when they were part of CVW-2's 1979 WestPac deployment. The squadron had actually started the decade within the same air wing aboard the same carrier, although their WestPac flying was anything but routine back in 1970, consisting mainly of strike missions into South Vietnam and Laos. VA-25 completed a total of six combat cruises aboard four different carriers between 1965 and 1973 — three with the Skyraider and three with the Corsair II. The squadron was redesignated VFA-25 on 1 July 1983 and issued with F/A-18As four months later, thus becoming only the second frontline unit in the Navy to receive the new generation light strike combat aircraft up to that point in time

**Above** A full 'court' of 'Royal Maces' from VA-27 enjoy a break during a squadron stand-down period in May 1979 at Lemoore. Heading up this ragged formation is a decidedly non-operational A-7E, the gaping hole left by the missing engine bay covers denoting that BuNo 156844's Allison TF41-A-2 turbofan powerplant has been removed for a lengthy period of maintenance in the squadron's engine shop. The variation in unit markings worn by these Corsair IIs was typical of the transitionary period between fully blown squadron colours and subdued TPS greys experienced by the light strike community from 1979 to 1984. Although eight of the 13 Corsairs II illustrated here appear to have lost the green fin cap and rudder triangles, all of the jets still wear full colour national markings and warning stencils. The squadron 'CAG Bird' carries the traditional 'double nuts'

00 modex on its fin cap as well as representative air wing shades on its rudder. VA-27 was attached to CVW-14 and the *Coral Sea* at the time, although as this photograph bears testament to, the squadron were six months away from their next WestPac, hence the lack of ramp activity. Along with sister-squadron VA-97 'Warhawks', the 'Royal Maces' flew A-7s in fleet service longer than any other squadron, having first transitioned onto the A-7A at Lemoore in September 1967. Twenty-three years and 14 WestPacs (including five to Vietnam) later, the squadron finally retired their A-7E 'Harleys' to Davis-Monthan, and received F/A-18Cs in their place. Today, the squadron is controlled by CVW-15 and when not at Lemoore calls the veteran flightdeck of *Kitty Hawk* home

**Below** Like VA-27, the 'Bulls' of VA-37 were established specifically to fly the Corsair II, the unit being declared operational on 1 December 1967. By the time this 'Bull' was photographed on long finals to Cecil Field in April 1980, the squadron had accrued considerable experience on the 'SLUF' during both war and peacetime cruises. Twelve months after VA-37 was declared operational they embarked aboard *Kitty Hawk* and headed for the war zone. Three AirLant deployments aboard USS *Saratoga* (CV-60) were completed during 1970/71, followed up by a bitter Task Force 77 cruise during *Linebacker I* and *II*. A total of 2600 combat missions were flown whilst the carrier spent 173 days on the line in the Tonkin Gulf, the 'Bulls' dropping 3100 tons of ordnance on a variety of targets but at some considerable cost in lives and equipment – four aircraft were lost to SAMs and AAA and two pilots killed. VA-37 traded in the battle weary A-7As for Echo models in December 1973 at Cecil Field,

the squadron then spending the next 17 years performing a steady cycle of Mediterranean and Atlantic deployments with a series of carriers assigned to the 6th Fleet. Now equipped with F/A-18Cs, VFA-37 are still tasked with AirLant duties as part of CVW-3 aboard USS *John F Kennedy* (CV-67). Equipped with empty bomb ejector racks of varying sizes on both wing hardpoints, this grubby 'Bull' was spotted returning from a short close air support (CAS) training sortie flown over the well-used Pinecastle range not too far from Cecil Field. VA-37 performed CAS duties with MAG-12 for six months in 1984/85 at MCAS Iwakuni as part of the two-year Marine Corps Unit Deployment Program, which saw four Corsair II squadrons spend six months each assigned to the Third Marine Air Wing. This highly unusual series of deployments was instigated by the Navy to make up for their own use of USMC A-6 and F/A-18 squadrons within Pacific and Atlantic fleet carrier air wings

**Right** One outfit that failed to make the transition from Corsair IIs to Hornets was VA-72 'Blue Hawks', this historically significant squadron being chopped on 30 June 1991 following the departure of their last A-7Es to Arizona. Six months earlier the squadron had been writing the final chapter of the Corsair II's naval career as it waged war alongside fellow 'SLUF' devotees VA-46 'Clansmen' during *Desert Storm*. This was the third time in just under 40 years that the unit had taken up arms against enemy forces, the squadron's initial blooding in action occuring over Korea in 1952/53 during a single combat deployment as VF-72 whilst equipped with F9F-2 Panthers and assigned to CVG-7 aboard *Bon Homme Richard*. Redesignated an attack squadron in the fall of 1955, the squadron went on to become the first frontline unit in the Navy to pick up A4D-1s when a factory-fresh airframe arrived at their NAS Quonset Point, Rhode Island, base in October 1956 – actually nicknamed the 'Sky Hawks' prior to the A4D's arrival, VA-72 quickly adopted the 'Blue' appellation to avoid any confusion. A move to NAS Oceana, Virginia, followed in 1957, as well as assignment to USS *Randolph* (CVA-15). After participating in USS *Independence's* (CV-62) shakedown cruise in April 1959, the squadron went on to perform several AirLant deployments to the Med with this vessel, before ending its association with CVW-7 and *'Indy'* following a long and bitter war cruise in the Tonkin Gulf in 1965. Whilst ashore, the 'Blue Hawks' moved further south to the growing AirLant attack facility at Cecil Field, the squadron barely having time to settle into its new surroundings before departing Mayport aboard USS *Franklin D Roosevelt* (CVA-42) on 21 June 1966, bound once again for Task Force 77. By the time the 'Blue Hawks' returned to Florida exactly eight months later the squadron had lost three A-4Es in combat, although two aircrew had to be rescued and the third made a POW. No more combat deployments were thrust upon VA-72 following their *'FDR'* WestPac, the unit settling down to the pre-war routine of Med cruises in support of NATO forces. The 'Blue Hawks' were one of 11(!) Skyhawk squadrons to transition onto the Corsair II in 1970, the unit embarking their A-7Bs aboard *John F Kennedy* in September 1970 for a 6th Fleet cruise as part of CVW-1. A-7Es replaced the underpowered Bravoes in 1977 whilst the squadron was still attached to *'JFK'* and CVW-1 – the unit renewed its association with CV-67 as part of CVW-3 in time to perform the Corsair II's last active carrier deployment (August 1990 to March 1991) in association with VA-46, during which time the squadron flew 362 combat sorties over Iraq and Kuwait, delivering over a million pounds of ordnance in the process. Wearing VA-72's pre-TPS scheme, this scuffed up A-7E was photographed as it passed through Hill AFB in September 1981 on a cross-country from Fallon to Cecil Field; note the maps poked down the side of the instrument coaming

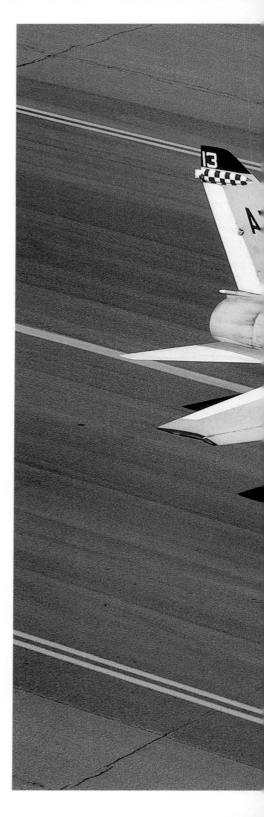

**Above** Canopy cranked open to keep the cockpit cool in the warm spring sun, 'Mighty Shrike 301' sits on the Lemoore ramp in May 1979 whilst a pair of VA-22 jets taxy past. Like the 'Redcocks', VA-94 earnt their battle spurs firstly in Korea with the F4U-4 Corsair aboard USS *Philippine Sea* in 1952/53 as a fighter squadron (VF-22 flew F2H-2 Banshees from USS *Lake Champlain* (CVA-39) in 1953), then as a fully-fledged attack unit equipped with A-4Cs 11 years later aboard the *Ranger*. A further seven combat cruises were undertaken over the following eight years, the final two in A-7Es aboard *Coral Sea* with CVV-15. A diet of six-monthly WestPacs was enjoyed by the 'Mighty Strikes' after the cessation of hostilities, the only real break in this routine occuring in April 1988 when VA-94, and the rest of CVW-11, participated in *Operation Preying Mantis* against the Iranian Navy in the Persian Gulf. From 1982 to 1990 the squadron's at sea home was the *Enterprise*, VA-94 transitioning onto Lot 12 F/A-18Cs at Lemoore soon after the '*Big E*' went into refit. Today, VFA-94 sail the world's oceans aboard USS *Abraham Lincoln* (CVN-72)

**Above** As the AirPac A-7 fleet replacement squadron (FRS), VA-122 operated the largest force of Corsair IIs at Lemoore – 24 airframes comprising both TA-7Cs and A-7Es. All of the unit's aircraft were worked hard by the classes passing through the FRS syllabus, a pilot's conversion typically lasting between six to eight months. As a result of the virtually endless circuit bashing (Field Practice Carrier Landings – FCLPs – in Navy parlance), and periodic dets to Fallon, El Centro and various carriers for weapons delivery and at sea training, the squadron's aircrat tended to look decidedly worse for wear. One jet that received perhaps a little more 'TLC' than its fellow ramp mates at VA-122 was 'Eagle One', the CO's personal aircraft; woe betide any 'nugget' that dared scratch this aircraft! Never known for setting the standard for outlandish fin art, VA-122's Corsair IIs rarely wore much in the way of unit markings, bar a yellow strip across the fin tip. This jet was photographed at Lemoore in August 1982, the various yellow patches liberally plastered all over its airframe containing instructions for the trainee maintainers, who were also instructed by VA-122 before being sent to a fleet squadron. Prior to receiving A-7As in November 1966, the 'Flying Eagles' had flown Skyraiders in both a frontline and training capacity since 1950. During its 25-year association with the Corsair II, VA-122 graduated close to 5000 qualified 'SLUF' pilots into the fleet, many of whom went on to distinguish themselves in combat over Vietnam, the Persian Gulf, Kuwait and Iraq. Following the completion of their last course in February 1991, VA-122 despatched its remaining A-7s and TA-7s to Davis-Monthan and then promptly disbanded

**Above** In late 1969 VA-122 began receiving A-7Es from LTV, the Echoes at first supplanting and eventually replacing the A-7A/B/Cs then on strength with the squadron. The early model Corsairs IIs were passed on to the recently re-tasked VA-125 'Rough Raiders' (also at Lemoore) who had up until mid-1969 been churning out replacement A-4 pilots and maintainers for AirPac. One of the last units to pass through VA-122's conversion syllabus prior to the squadron's total embracing of the A-7E was VA-146 'Blue Diamonds', who traded in their war weary A-4Cs for new A-7Bs in late 1968. An ex-FJ-4B Fury squadron from the 1950s, VA-146 joined the massed Skyhawk ranks in the early 1960s and had completed several WestPacs with the type prior to Vietnam flaring up. Three combat tours in as many years with CVW-14 aboard *Constellation* (twice) and *Ranger* (once) gave the 'Blue Diamonds' as much combat experience as any light

strike unit at Lemoore up to that point in the conflict. Wise to the squadron's excessive exposure to the Vietnam War, and the obsolescence of their A-4Cs, AirPac decided that the 'Blue Diamonds' should spend 1968 transitioning onto the Corsair II. Following this brief respite from combat, VA-146 went on to perform a further four WestPacs with Task Force 77 (one with A-7Bs and three with A-7Es) as part of CVW-9. Postwar, the squadron continued to operate over the Pacific and Indian Oceans during regular six-monthly deployments aboard a variety of 3rd and 7th Fleet carriers. Up until the introduction of TPS greys in the early 1980s, VA-146's markings varied little from their Vietnam days, as this A-7E photograhed at Hill AFB in August 1976 shows. The squadron's association with the Corsair II ended in early 1989 when they welcomed the first of 15 brand new F/A-18C Hornets direct from St Louis

**Below** Two legends of the light strike world (okay, so this Skyhawk is a trainer version!) sit side by side on the Moffet Field', California, transient ramp in May 1974. Despite its well-used appearance, this A-7C is no more than four years old, the exposed deck environment endured by a fleet aircraft clearly taking its toll on the lustre of the grey and white scheme. The Charlie was LTV's transitionary model between the austere Alphas and Bravoes and the definitive Echoes, which eventually populated the lights strike world in abundance. The A-7C entered service with all the trick equipment developed for the A-7E like the General Electric M61A1 Vulcan cannon, anti-skid brakes, AN/AVQ-7(V) Head-Up Display (HUD), improved triple redundant hydraulic system for the flight controls, and perhaps most importantly the AN/ASN-91(V) Navigation/Weapons Delivery tactical computer and forward looking AN/AVQ-126(V) radar, which allowed the pilot to deliver his ordnance with pinpoint accuracy (both iron bombs and TV/optically guided weapons) in all but the worst weather conditions. However, due to development problems experienced by Allison with the definitive 15,000 lbs thrust rated TF41-A-2 turbofan, the Navy ordered LTV to fit the less powerful Pratt & Whitney TF30-P-408 (13,400 lbs) into the first 67 A-7Es, which were creating something of a traffic jam on the company's Dallas production line. Re-designated the A-7C, these aircraft were never re-engined, but 36 were later converted into two-seat TA-7Cs by LTV between 1975 and 1978

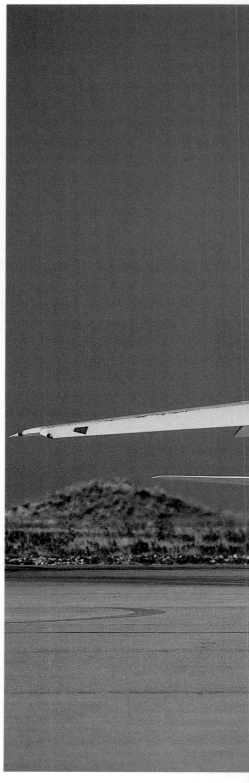

**Above and right** Unbelievable as it may seem, these two A-7Bs actually belong to the same squadron – VA-303 'Golden Hawks' – and the TPS-adorned jet was photographed five months before its colourful ramp mate! Along with fellow CVWR-30 members VA-304 'Firebirds', the 'Golden Hawks' were the first of six reserve manned light attack units to replace their Skyhawks with Corsair IIs, the transition occuring in 1971. Prior to flying the A-7A, VA-303 had operated F4U-4s and A-4Bs, the squadron having spent two decades in a decommissioned state following its initial postwar formation in 1946 with Vought's original 'bent-winged bird'. As the B-models were retired from frontline service in the late 1970s, so the three CVWR-20 units (VAs -303, -304 and -305) traded up to the Bravo. However, the increased capability bestowed upon the reserves by this version of the Corsair II was tempered for the squadron maintainers by the generally weary state of their 'new' jets, which had already experienced combat tours over Vietnam and countless postwar WestPacs. Photographed in October 1982 and February 1983 respectively, both aircraft carry practice bomb-configured TERs on the wing hardpoints. At the time, the squadron was in the process of clipping the 'Golden Hawk's' wings once and for all with a comprehensive coating of TPS greys. By the time VA-303 despatched its last A-7Bs to Davis-Monthan in late 1985 following the transferring of early-batch F/A-18As across the Lemoore ramp from VFA-125 to the reserve-manned unit, this once glorious scheme had long since disappeared

**Right** The third light attack squadron within CVWR-30 to receive A-7As was VA-305 'Lobos', who retired their A-4Es the year after VAs -303 and -304. Based just north of Los Angeles at NAS Point Mugu, the 'Lobos' performed all the regular training cycles practised on a full-time basis by their fleet brethren, including maintaining their carrier landing qualifications during annual two-week at sea deployments. Weapons work was also carried out as a matter of routine, the squadron benefiting from their close proximity to the immense instrumented ranges of the Pacific Missile Test Center off the coast of Point Mugu. Carrying a most unothodox stores fit beneath its large wing, this A-7A was photographed crossing the base perimeter fence following a multi-role mission in July 1976 out over the Pacific. Besides the two standard issue TERs, which undoubtedly carried Mk 76 'blue' bombs when the aircraft departed an hour before, this jet also boasts a D-704 refuelling pod on the port outer wing pylon and a dummy Martin Marietta AGM-62 Walleye guided missile on the reciprocal starboard hardpoint. A weapon developed specifically for the Navy in the early 1960s, over 4500 Walleye Is were produced between 1966 and 1970. Used extensively in Vietnam, the Walleye has been modified, rebuilt and upgraded through various programmes over the ensuing decades, the resulting weapons being given a variety of designations. Perhaps the ultimate AGM-62 is the Walleye IIER/DL (extended-range/datalink), over 100 of which were launched by A-7Es in the Gulf War. The weapon carried beneath the wing of the aircraft is a Walleye I (the original baseline version), which featured a TV seeker that required lock-on before launch and an 845 lb linear shaped-charge warhead. Although this device is inert, the TV seeker is still operable, thus allowing the pilot to practice his target lock-on techniques. VA-305 eventually retired their A-7As in 1978, the replacement B-models soldiering on until the arrival of F/A-18As at Point Mugu in January 1987

**These pages** One of the last users of the Corsair II as a 'crater creator' in Navy service was the Naval Strike Warfare Center (NSWC) at NAS Fallon, this vital command maintaining a small flight of six to eight A-7E/TA-7Cs to help in the continually evolving training syllabus developed at the Nevada base. Other types like the A-6E and F/A-18A were also adorned with the distinctive Strike lightning bolt at the same time, the NSWC fleet being put through its paces over the various instrumented ranges by seasoned pilots and NFOs posted to the unit following one or two frontline tours. Due to the realistic nature of the training required by visiting air wings undertaking the Strike Det syllabus, the NSWC flight is tasked with proving that the mission profiles built up by the dedicated warfare officers back at base are valid from both the safety and instructional points of view out over the various ranges. Working through his brief above the Bravo 20 site in September 1991 was seasoned light striker Lt Doug Merchant, his A-7E (armed-up with six 500 lb Mk 82 LDGPs with conical fins) performing one of the last live strike missions flown by the veteran Corsair II in Navy service. The first photograph in this unique sequence shows Doug pushing the A-7 almost through the vertical in a speed brake out dive from a Split-S manoeuvre – this radical attack profile was flown for photographic purposes only, as the negative G affecting the airframe near the vertical plane would hinder

safe separation of the bombs from the hardpoints. Restored to a more orthodox attack attitude, Lt Merchant 'pickles' his 'slicks' whilst in a 20° dive at about 7000 ft above the target, a height recognised as being well out of shoulder SAM and small-arms fire range. Soon after releasing his ordnance, Lt Merchant experienced chronic hydraulic failure in his A-7E and he had to rapidly dump fuel before performing an emergency recovery back at Fallon

**Above** Photoship for the unforgettable Fallon mission was an NSWC TA-7C capably flown by the flight's boss, Cdr Loving. About half a dozen 'two holers' were maitained by the unit to perform 'fastFAC' and NFO training tasks, as well as communication and general 'hack 'work. The briefed 'hard deck' altitude for this mission was 'tumbleweed' height judging by this unique self-portrait

**Right** Photographed just seconds away from landing at NAS Patuxant River, Maryland, during September 1979, this distinctively marked A-7E actually hailed from Naval Weapons Center China Lake in the heart of California, hence the garish external tanks. In this cross-country configuration the Corsair II was capable of covering 2861 miles with the aid of external tanks. VX-5 'Vampires' are one of three test and evaluation squadrons within the Navy, this particular unit's speciality being the operational development of strike aircraft, and the weapons and tactics adopted in association with these frontline types by the fleet. With such a broad brief, the 'Vampires' have been in the envious position of trialling all the Navy/Marine service types prior to them being cleared for operational use. Formed on 18 June 1957, VX-5 was heavily involved in weapons clearance work for the Corsair II a decade later as the aircraft was prepared for its combat debut over Vietnam in the hands of VA-147 'Argonauts'. With the introduction of updated versions of the Corsair II, VX-5 was kept busy proving that the new modifications to the airframe met the rigorous fleet-level requirements. Similarly, new weapons and external avionics like the FLIR pod all had to be exhaustively tested and cleared for service use. Along with the Strike Aircraft Test Directorate fleet at Pax River, VX-5's A-7Es retained the traditional white and grey scheme through to their collective retirement in early 1992

**Above and right** When a time of crisis arises and the various frontline units of the fleet are expected to put ordnance on targets at short notice in any weather, the last thing the CAG needs to be worrying about is the reliability of his weaponry, and its ability to perform as its manufacturers have claimed. In between Martin Marietta, Hughes or Ford Aerospace developing a piece of equipment, trialling it and then selling the device to the Navy, and the squadron armourers bolting the bomb, missile or rocket onto the aircraft whilst is sits shackled to the steel deck of the carrier, the operators of these Corsair IIs will have thoroughly evaluated it first. Wearing the strongly Indian-flavoured eagle motif on their fins, as well as a suitably verbose naval acronym (which clearly lends itself to being applied incorrectly by the flight paintshop), these aircraft were photographed in the early 1980s at the Naval Weapons Evaluation Facility's Kirtland AFB home in New Mexico. Established a decade earlier to support work carried out jointly by the USAF and USN with regards to the delivery methods of nuclear and conventional warloads, the Corsair IIs flew alongside NAVWPNEVALFAC A-6Es until being replaced in the late 1980s by F/A-18s. The extremely tired looking A-7C was photographed in April 1980, the black line running aft below the wing from right of the faded 'star and bar' helping to give the camera footage shot from a chasing aircraft a constant reference point for weapons release calculations. In contrast to its flight mate, the TA-7C looked brand new when it was photographed in March 1982 – this particular airframe initially entered fleet service as an A-7C, before being sent to LTV in July 1977 for conversion. A close look at the pilot's helmet reveals the letters 'XO' on its rear, thus denoting that the driver of said Corsair II was in fact the flight's deputy commander

**Above** Another ancillary Corsair II operator was VAQ-34 'Flashbacks', who were formerly known as the 'Electric Horsemen' prior to the arrival of female naval aviators and NFOs at the unit in the late 1980s. Part of the Fleet Electronic Warfare Support Group (FEWSG), the squadron's primary task is to train land-based and shipboard radar systems operators in the art of tracking hostile aircraft, and combat the associated electronic jamming devices these aircraft can employ to mask their positions. Only established as recently as 1 March 1983, VAQ-34 was one of the last units to receive the Corsair II. In fact, a brand new variant of the aircraft was specially created to fulfil the unit's specialized role, six suitably modified TA-7Cs (redesignated EA-7Ls) entering service at Point Mugu 18 months after VAQ-34 was commissioned. Towards the end of the Corsair II's service career, a handful of elderly A-7Es were also transferred to the squadron from the recently transitioned strike fighter units at Lemoore. The only modification performed by VAQ-34 to the aircraft prior to them being cleared for the FEWSG mission was the deletion of the previous squadron markings in favour of a 'Flashbacks' red star and modex; this 'half-hour' conversion is perfectly illustrated by BuNo 160000, photographed in July 1991 sitting on the tyre-marked threshold at Lemoore prior to commencing a training sortie. The pilot on this flight was VAQ-34's XO, Cdr Chuck Swartzbach

**Right** Cruising over the patchwork fields of the San Joaquin Valley, a brace of Corsairs from different generations hold formation for the benefit of the camera. The pristine F4U-5N is privately owned by Dick Bretea, who has restored the Corsair in the colours of its former owners, VMF-451 'Warlords' – today's VMFA-451 are equipped with F/A-18Cs, and call MCAS Beaufort, South Carolina, home

**Above** Looking about as blotchy as any A-7 possibly could, BuNo 160000 cruises over Lemoore prior to breaking hard left into the landing pattern. Showing off for the camera, Cdr Swartzbach has deployed the aircraft's large ventral airbrake, which was designed by LTV to assist the pilot in manoeuvring the Corsair II during low-level attack missions without a noticeable trim change or excessive buffeting. The brake itself is made up of a long central plate which is flanked by pivoted side panels. This particular airframe was one of three A-7Es transferred to VAQ-34 from VFA-27 following the latter squadron's re-equipment with F/A-18Cs in the autumn of 1990. A close inspection of the red titling below the cockpit reveals the name of Cdr Rosemary Mariner, the unit's commanding officer

**Right** With the F4U-5N having departed due to a lack of avgas, Cdr Swartzbach continues his trip back through the light strike 'hall of fame' by slotting into this even more unusual formation. Leading the quartet in his burbling AD-5 Skyraider is Col Don Hanna (USMC ret), whilst to his left is a suitably camouflaged VFA-127 'Cylons' A-4E from NAS Fallon. Keeping a firm visible lock-on to the three jets above him, the boss of VFA-27, Cdr DP Davis, cruises along in the slot position strapped into the 'Royal Mace's' CVW-15 CAG bird

**Left** Judging by the hasty respraying of the tails of these weathered EA-7Ls, they too were recently posted to VAQ-34 from another unit, possibly the former A-7 training squadron VA-122. The 'Flashbacks' were formed specifically to provide permanent EW training to Pacific Fleet assets following the FEWSG decision that VAQ-33 'Firebirds', based at Key West in Florida, could not physically fulfil the role from their East Coast base. The latter unit had up until 1983 provided training for all fleet assets using modified TA-4Fs (EA-4Fs) and EA-3Bs. When it came time to activate a second FEWSG unit it was found that insufficient Skyhawks existed for modification, so six TA-7Cs were rebuilt with new wiring looms, which enabled them to carry five different EW/jammer/emitter pods. Cockpit displays were also modified accordingly to enable the NFO to quickly manipulate the stores to vary the training profiles to suit the task at hand. Late in the 1980s several former VA-176 'Hellrazors' TA-7Cs were modified to EA-7L standard and issued to VAQ-33 as EA-4F replacements. All FEWSG EA-7s were finally retired in early 1992 as surplus early-build F/A-18A/Bs became available

**Above** Wearing distinctive LTV house colours, the one-off YA-7E glides over the Dallas Airport perimeter bound for a routine recovery back at the huge Texas field in April 1985. Owner of three separate designations during its long flying career, BuNo 156801 initially started life as the very first full-spec A-7E built by LTV for the Navy. Returned almost immediately to the manufaturers, the airframe was used as a flying test bed for various mods and upgrades carried out by LTV to Navy order. Heavily modified in early 1972 into the prototype 'Twosair', the longer (by three feet) and heavier (500 lbs) YA-7H, as it was then designated, first flew from Dallas in the hands of test pilot John Konrad on 29 August 1972. Retaining all its single-seat offensive capabilities and internal fuel, the YA-7H was informally tested by the instructors at VA-122, who praised it so thoroughly that LTV put a formal proposal for immediate manufacture forward to the CNO. In typically frugal style, the Navy decided to convert surplus Bravo and Charlie model aircraft into two-seaters, rather than spend large sums of money on new-build airframes. At about the same time as BuNo 156801 was undergoing evaluation, the sale of Corsair IIs to Greece was confirmed, and their Echo-standard A-7Hs (H for Hellenic) began rolling down the Dallas line. To avoid designation confusion, the solitary YA-7H became a YA-7E, and although service two-seaters flew as TA-7Cs with the Navy, the civilian-operated BuNo 156801 retained its Echo-model handle

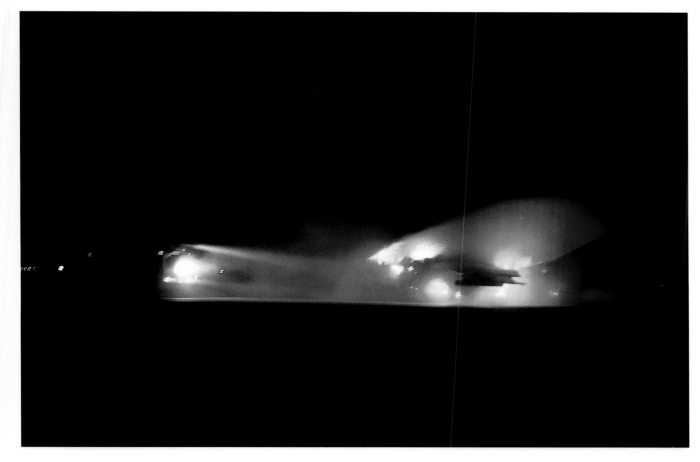

**Above** Doing its best 'Joan of Arc meets Guy Fawkes' night impression, the Fallon fire section successfully reduce the Navy's number of surplus TA-7Cs by one. This fate has befallen dozens of struck-off Corsair IIs at various naval air stations across the US over the past four years

# AV-8tor – Harrier II

**Right** When the US Marine Corps initiated a study into a replacement for its A-4s in the late 1960s, many defence analysts in Washngton automatically assumed that the 'leathernecks' would follow the Navy lead and buy A-7 Corsair IIs in bulk. However, senior Corps personnel were adamant that they wanted an aircraft that could literally come ashore with the troops virtually from day one, and support the 'grunt' in hand-to-hand combat at very short notice. Although the Corsair II possessed long legs and could tote a handy bomb load, it was badly hamstrung by its conventional catapult launch and arrestor recovery traits. The USMC's unique requirements caught the American aerospace industry on the back foot, and with little on offer on home turf, the Corps cast their eyes 'across the pond' to Britain. Here, the Harrier GR.1 was just entering RAF service, having reached the production stage after a politically difficult gestation period. The aircraft was initially evaluated by the Americans at the 1968 Farnborough Air Show, the Corps' enthusiasm for the type eventually forcing the US government to strike a deal with Hawkers for the Harrier to be licence-built as the AV-8A by McDonnell Douglas on 23 December 1969. However, due to the rigid fiscal year procurement cycle utilized by the Americans, the orders for the AV-8 were never large enough to warrant the opening of a production line in St Louis, so all 110 aircraft were built by the British at Kingston, in Surrey, and airfreighted to the US; when this photograph was taken at Maxwell AFB, Alabama, in September 1974, the last batch of Harriers were in the process of being delivered to the USMC. Three frontline squadrons and a single training unit flew the AV-8A, this virtually zero-hour airframe belonging to VMA-231 'Aces' of Cherry Point, who were in fact the last Harrier squadron formed on the early model aircraft. Devoid of the unit's familiar ace of spades playing card motif in the black circle beneath the cockpit, the jet's occupant is, however, wearing an appropriately decorated bonedome. Initially activated with the Harrier on 15 May 1973, the squadron was nearing the end of its combat crew readiness training when this aircraft was photographed, VMA-231 achieving its carrier qualifications aboard USS *Inchon* (LPH-12) the following January. After a det to Puerto Rico in September 1976, the 'Aces' embarked their full complement of 14 aircraft aboard *Franklin D Roosevelt* and participated in the fixed-wing carrier's last Med cruise. The six-month long deployment proved beyond a doubt that the Harrier could be seamlessly integrated into the carrier air wing, although no mixed CVWs have put to sea since. Over the next seven years the squadron successfully flew the AV-8A in a variety of exercises across Europe and South-east Asia, as well as establishing a permanent det at Kadena, in Okinawa. In September 1984, following in-theatre work off the coast of the Lebanon and Norway aboard various LPHs and LHAs, VMA-231 returned to Cherry Point and commenced its transition onto the AV-8B

**Above** Built within the same 30-aircraft batch as the VMA-231 AV-8A, this scruffy looking Harrier had, however, seen a further eight years of service by the time it was captured on celluloid for posterity at MCAS Yuma in August 1982. Assigned to the first Harrier unit in the Corps, this aircraft was reworked into an AV-8C soon after this photograph was taken, at the Naval Air Rework Center at Cherry Point – the mod allowed it to soldier on with VMA-513 'Flying Nightmares' until the squadron re-equipped with AV-8Bs in January 1987. Sixteen years earlier, the 'Flying Nightmares' had just commenced work-ups on the Corps' first AV-8As at MCAS Beaufort, the squadron having previously flown the F-4B over Vietnam as VMFA-513. Trailblazing with the Harrier, the squadron cleared the type for ordnance delivery at China Lake in the autumn of 1971, as well as performing carquals aboard USS *Guadalcanal* (LPH-7) and USS *Coronado* (LPD-11). Full 'blue water' deployments soon followed, as well as establishing the first Far East det with MAG-12 at MCAS Iwakuni. Home-base shifted to Cherry Point in 1976, and VMA-513 maintained its schedule of regular sea time and Far East tours of duty for the rest of the decade. In 1984 the squadron moved from MAG-32 to MAG-13 at Yuma, the 'Flying Nightmares' being the sole V/STOL exponents in the air group until the last A-4Ms were retired in 1989/90 – by this stage the squadron had become seasoned AV-8B exponents

**Above right** The Harrier II is essentially a totally new aircraft that bears only a superficial resemblance to its progenitor, as this view across the Cherry Point ramp in November 1992 clearly shows. Sitting side-by-side on the VMA-223 'Bulldogs' line (note the distinctive squadron emblem on the hangar wall), today's AV-8B shares the same concrete with yesterday's AV-8C; the weather-beaten Harrier clings on to the last vestiges of a VMA-231 'Aces' black roundel beneath the cockpit, thus giving it some form of

identity. The AV-8B, on the other hand, is totally devoid of any distinguishing marks, the 'Bulldogs' only applying the boxing canine motif to the starboard side of their jets. A former A-4M squadron, VMA-223 have flown Harrier IIs with MAG-32 since 1987, the unit recently upgrading to the AV-8B(NA)

**Below right** Father of all Harrier IIs is this decidedly non-combat configured AV-8B (BuNo 161396), which is seen 'catching some rays' at Edwards on 6 December 1984. Built as the first of four full-scale development (PSD) aircraft ordered by the USMC in 1979 following trials with two hybrid YAV-8B aerodynamic prototypes (AV-8As fitted with the new B-model wing), the aircraft first flew from St Louis on 26 February 1981. It was eventually joined by the remaining three PSD AV-8Bs, as well as the two YAV-8Bs, and despatched firstly to Pax River for service testing and then to Edwards for further systems trials work. By the time this shot was taken, the bulk of the important Marine acceptance work had been successfully completed, and the first 11 AV-8Bs handed over to VMAT-203 at Cherry Point. As is always the case with trials aircraft, this particular airframe has been maintained in spotless condition, its Corps flavoured scheme radiating in the warm winter sun. One of the YAV-8Bs was passed on to NASA in the late 1980s for V/STOL research work in California, whilst the four FSD airframes continue to perform trials work in association with the programme

**Above** Sharing ramp space with FSD 1 on that December day was FSD 3 (BuNo 161398), which wore a hybrid service/test scheme specifically applied for the trials work it was then carrying out at Edwards. A quick glance at the AV-8B's tail reveals the nature of its work – spin recovery testing. The rather 'agricultural' tubing securely bolted to the aircraft's modified tail boom supports the vital drag chute cannister which would deploy its contents should the AV-8 enter an uncontrollable spin. The orange and white paint was applied to the flying surfaces to allow observers (both on the ground and in the air) to keep track of the aircraft's attitude and height. Following the successful completion of the tests the aircraft was returned to its more conventional configuration. Unlike FSD 1, this airframe still has the original double row of intake suction relief doors as fitted to the first 16 AV-8Bs that entered service. Also noteworthy is the heraldic nameplate for McAir test pilot Bill Lowe beneath the cockpit. Having first flown in April 1982, FSD 3 was initially tasked with avionics and weapons integration trials prior to arriving at Edwards for spin tests

**Right** A close-up of FSD 3's inlet doors, photographed with the engine shut down between sorties. The original single-row eight slot intakes of the AV-8A were modified by McDonnell Douglas to cope with the demands placed on the airflow by the new Pegasus II engine fitted to the AV-8B, their number being increased to twelve, split in two rows of six. However, McAir technicians were not satisfied with the arrangement, and after round-the-clock work by a team of 500 specialists at St Louis, the layout was changed and the definitive aircraft emerged with a single row of seven larger doors per intake. This minor alteration boosted the AV-8B's engine thrust by about 600 lbs, improving the aircraft's low-altitude high-speed performance, as well as its acceleration. The doors suck inwards when the pilot slows down into the hover, allowing the engine to ingest more air so as to make up for the lack of forced airflow. When the pilot transitions back to conventional flight, the airflow forced through the intakes increases accordingly and the extra 'lung capacity' afforded the engine by the intakes is no longer necessary, so they automatically close when the speed change is sensed

**Left and right** Contrasting cockpits. The 'office' to the left belongs to a basic 'vanilla' AV-8B, the single Kaiser IPI318/A multi-function display Digital Data Indicator being positioned to the left of the cockpit. Immediately below the Smiths Industries SU-128/A HUD is the all-important up-front-controller panel, which is used by the pilot to programme the majority of the systems aboard the aircraft. The chunky control column is festooned with switches for the trim, target selection/designation equipment, radios, chaff and flare dispensers, gun firing and weapons release. The cockpit to the right features a second multi-function display, which is slaved to a Honeywell colour digital moving map. This system has been installed in the AV-8B Night Attack (NA) variant, which is now in service with all four Yuma-based Harrier II squadrons. The displaced manual fuel flow and nozzle temperature displays which previously occupied the right hand side of the console have been fitted around the TV screen in the AV-8B(NA), with the remainder of the cockpit being left untouched. The ergonomic and generally spacious feel of the Harrier II's cockpit greatly impressed seasoned 'AV-8tors' from the cramped Alpha and Charlie model era, the pilots enjoying the 'easier to read' instruments and the higher seat pitch adopted by McAir engineers

**Above left** The offensive portion of the AV-8B's twin-pod General Electric GAU-12/U Equaliser 25 mm cannon fit. Driven by a pneumatic motor turned at 9000 rpm by engine bleed air and geared down to the rear of the weapons pod, the GAU-12/U is capable of firing 3600 round per minute. Fed from a dedicated 300 round magazine pod across a bridge (which also acts as a lift improvement device), the five-barrel weapon proved extremely effective at 'keeping heads down' during strike missions in the Gulf War

**Below left** The magazine fairing is of identical proportions to the cannon pod, its interior being packed with a linkless feed system which holds 300 rounds of 25 mm ammunition of armour-piercing incendiary, armour-piercing discarding sabot, high explosive incendiary or training round construction. As can be seen in this chapter, squadrons tend not to fit the pods for routine flying unless gun training is specified on the daily orders

**Above** First stop for Corps pilots destined for a frontline Harrier II posting is UMAT-203 'Hawks', the USMC's sole AV-8 training squadron. Based at Cherry Point, the 'Hawks' control the largest force of Harrier IIs in the Corps, their fleet including all three types of V/STOL jet currently being operated in frontline service. The dedicated TAV-8B is by far the most important version on the squadron books, the 'Hawks' controlling almost all of the 28 'two-holers' ordered by the Corps for training purposes. VMAT-203 was infact the last squadron to retire the veteran Harrier 'I' from the Marine Corps, their weary TAV-8As being forced to serve on as initial conversion trainers for the AV-8B whilst the dedicated TAV-8B was flight tested prior to delivery. The last TAV-8As left Cherry Point as late as November 1987 following VMAT-203's work-ups with the twin-stick Bravo; the first all-TAV-8B class graduated from Cherry Point in the spring of 1988. Photographed outside the 'Hawks' suitably coded hangar in November 1992, two relatively new TAV-8Bs sit alongside an older airframe that is still sprayed up in its original wraparound grey/green delivery scheme

**Above** Besides the two-seaters, VMAT-203 also operates over a dozen
AV-8Bs of varying ages, as well as a handful of AV-8B(NA)s. One of the older
Harrier IIs at Cherry Point, BuNo 162948 has recently adopted the
fashionable soft grey scheme which is reapidly appearing on all Corps AV-8s.
The shades of grey used bear a striking resemblance to the colours worn on
McAir's FSD 4 Harrier II, which first flew from St Louis back in June 1983 –
colour schemes do have a habit of coming full circle! Cruising over the lush
wetlands of North Carolina following the successful execution of a planned
bombing sortie, the student pilot formates with a 'Hawks' TAV-8B for a brief
photo session before recovering back at Cherry Point

**Right** AV-8B meat in a TAV-8B sandwich, the pilot gesticulates towards the
author as the three-ship cruises over North Carolina at a much greater height
than in the previous photograph. Both aircraft are carrying empty TERs
configured for Mk 76 bombs, and the AV-8B also boasts an equally barren
LAU-105 Sidewinder launch rail. During *Desert Storm* AV-8Bs rarely used
bulky TERs after the first few days of the fighting, squadrons preferring to
mount single bombs to individual pylons, thus keeping the weight and
airflow disturbances associated with external ordnance to a bare minimum.
Maintaining the VMAT-203 tradition of tailcodes and modex numbers being
applied in white , 'Hawk 30' contrasts markedly with its much newer
squadron mate. The repainting of the avionics bay access panel also suggests
that either BuNo 162948 has recently been issued to VMAT-203 from another
squadron, or that the cover itself has been 'borrowed' from a sister-unit

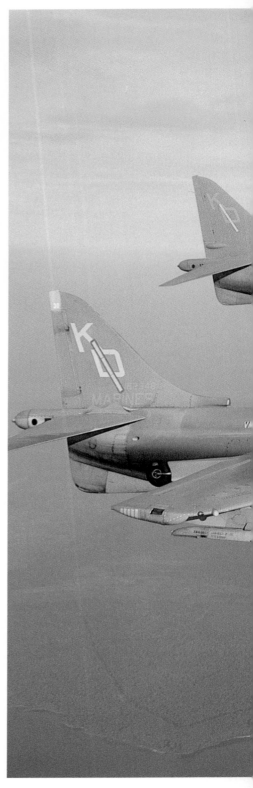

**Above** Same twin, different single. Hot on 'Hawk 30's' heels as it rolled down the St Louis production line in 1985 was 'Hawk 34', both aircraft being duly despatched to Cherry Point following their pre-delivery flight checks. Wearing identical camouflage schemes, BuNo 162949 stands apart from its older brother by having a low-viz nose modex, despite the white squadron codes and titling on its fuselage and tail. The VMAT-203 course at Cherry Point lasts 22 weeks and sees the pilot graduate with 60 hours of AV-8B/TAV-8B stick time in his log book. He will leave the 'Hawks' with a 'combat-capable' rating, which is then upgraded to 'combat-ready' status after the pilot has passed strenuous frontline squadron training cycles

**Left** The first TAV-8B flew from St Louis in October 1986, BuNo 162747 being the 67th Harrier II built up to that point in the programme. The Marines made sure they ordered the two-seater early to avoid a repeat of the unacceptable losses incurred in the early 1970s by pilots converting onto the AV-8A without the benefit of dual-seat training time – the first TAV-8A did not entire service until 1976, well after the last batch of AV-8As had been issued to frontline units. In those days, VMAT-203 taught most of its syllabus on TA-4s, the pilots acquiring limited experience of V/TOL by notching up four to five hours in the right-hand seat of a CH-46 Sea Knight! Having flown conventional fixed-wing types like the Skyhawk and Phantom II for most of their service lives, the recently converted 'AV-8tors' found the Harrier quite a handful in the V/STOL phase of its flight envelope, and as a result the three frontline squadrons suffered the worst accident rates of any fixed-wing operators in the USMC in the years up to the introduction of the TAV-8A

WARNING
HIS AIRCRAFT CONTAINS A CARTRIDGE-
TUATED EMERGENCY ESCAPE SYSTEM
UIPPED WITH EXPLOSIVE CHARGES.
PLICABLE MAINTENANCE MANUAL

DANGER
EJECTION SEAT
&
CANOPY
DANGER    DANGER

MA

**Above** For many years the standard colours worn by Harrier IIs, the now rarely seen grey/green 'jungle' scheme has been widely replaced by a variety of different ghost grey shades which seem to vary from squadron to squadron. Deployment to the Gulf for participation in *Desert Storm* sounded the death-knell for the older scheme, as several of the squadrons called up for duty in the Gulf unofficially took it upon themselves to respray their jets in a combination of colours which best rendered them 'invisible' in the hazy skies of the Middle East. McDonnell Douglas soon added an air of permanency to the predominance of 'ghostly' AV-8Bs when it began delivering brand new Night Attack Harrier IIs in a solid grey shade, which they claimed reduced the aircraft's infrared (IR) signature. Photographed in the days when 'real' Harrier IIs wore jungle shades, this FY 1985 airframe from VMA-513 was seen carrying an AIM-9L acquisition round on its port missile pylon in June 1989

**Left** Sitting pretty on his Stencel S111S-3AV8B zero-zero ejection seat, a seasoned 'leatherneck' protects his eyes from the sun's glare by rolling down the tinted plexiglass visor from within his bonedone. Whilst his Rolls-Royce F402-RR-408 turbofan purrs away, the pilot systematically runs through his BIT (Built-in Test) checks, which scour the aircraft's black boxes for glitches, and then aligns his Litton AN/ASN-130A intertial navigation system (INS). Now he can sit back and wait for the other pilots in his flight to complete their checks, before receiving the signal over his comms set that they are ready to roll. Behind the pilot's head is the miniature detonating cord (MDC), which shatters the canopy immediately after the pilot has initiated the ejection sequence, and milli-seconds prior to the seat punching out of the cockpit

**Above left** Internal tanks topped off, a weathered AV-8B from VMA-542 'Flying Tigers' drops back behind the drogue of a KC-130F and prepares to resume its transpac to MCAS Iwakuni. Photographed in December 1989, this aircraft was one of a dozen Harrier IIs that left MCAS Cherry Point bound for MAG-12 as part of VMA-542's first rotational period in Japan with the AV-8B. Lightened as much as possible prior to the flight (note the lack of underwing stores or GAU-12 cannon pods), the aircraft has been plumbed with the largest size of external tank available to the AV-8B; VMA-542 returned to Cherry Point in June 1990, their MAG-12 slot being filled by VMA-231 'Aces'. However, both units were soon to meet up again as part of the Marine's contribution to *Desert Shield/Storm,* the 'Flying Tigers' being one of the first units to arrive in-theatre following the call to arms. Based at King Abdul Aziz Airfield, Saudi Arabia, from 23 August 1990, the squadron commandeered a local soccer stadium, and its parking lot, and flew operations over Kuwait from here for the next eight months. Led into battle by Lt Col Ted Herman, VMA-542 were assigned a variety of tasks

once the shooting war commenced, including the destruction of rocket launchers, artillery pieces and FROG missiles, as well as performing armed reconnaissance sorties over 15 by 15 mile sectors of southern Kuwait, where the pilots were cleared to hit any 'targets of opportunity'. When the Allies rolled into Kuwait and Iraq as part of the *Desert Sabre* operation, the 'Flying Tigers' switched specifically to anti-armour missions, this change in tasking eventually resulting in the squadron losing two AV-8Bs (one pilot was killed and the other safely ejected) to hand-held SAMs. Following the conclusion of the conflict in March 1991, VMA-542 soon returned to Cherry Point and routine peace-time flying. Initially formed as a dedicated night fighter unit in August 1944 and equipped with F6F-5N Hellcats, VMF(N)-542, as it was then designated, went on to serve in two conflicts following the end of World War 2 – it flew F7F-3N Tigercats over Korea, and just over a decade later performed strike missions from Da Nang equipped with F-4B Phantom IIs. Pulled out of the war zone in 1969 and sent back to El Toro, VMFA-542 deactivated a year

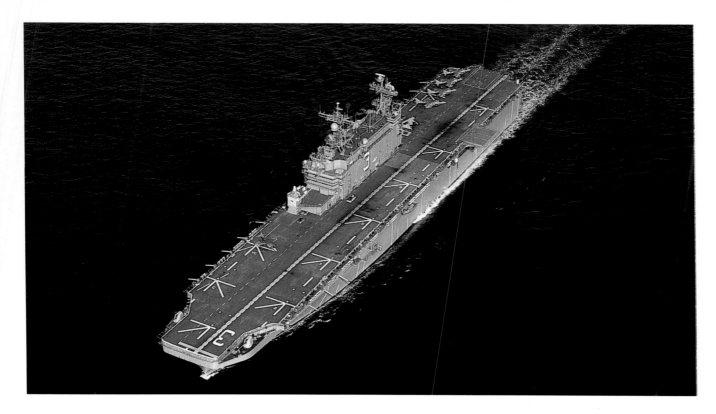

later, and whilst operationally dormant moved coasts to MCAS Beaufort. Now part of MAG-32, VMA-542 was commissioned on 1 November 1972 as the second AV-8A unit in the Corps. After 14 years of service across the globe, the 'Flying Tigers' retired their AV-8A/Cs to Davis-Monthan in 1986, and received AV-8B Harrier IIs in their place

**Above right** The US Navy's steel equivalent of a Marine Corps Air Station is a 40,000 ton assault carrier of the *Tarawa* or *Wasp* classes, these multi-purpose vessels also serving as floating docks for landing craft. Although the Corps' AV-8As initially went to sea aboard the smaller 18,000 ton *Iwo Jima* class assault carriers in the mid-1970s, the cramped deck space of these LPHs soon convinced the Navy that they needed a larger vessel from which to safely operate a mixed force of Harriers and helicopters – thus, the LHA was developed. Wearing a large '3' on its island, this vessel was commissioned as USS *Belleau Wood* (LHA-3) on 23 September 1978, the third LHA in a five-

ship class. Capable of embarking between 35 and 40 aircraft, the assault carrier is the main weapon of power projection available to the Corps, its unparalleled ability to land and support troops tasked with establishing a beach-head having been proven in numerous exercises across the globe. Initially rarely seen on WestPac or AirLant cruises aboard these ships, the AV-8B has increasingly become an integral part of most LHA/LHD Marine air wings over the past five years. Like their fixed-wing Navy brethren, Harrier II pilots have to complete pre-cruise work-ups prior to embarking on an operational deployment. In March 1992, VMA-211 'Wake Island Avengers' flew six AV-8B(NA)s out to *Belleau Wood* from Yuma for a week of concentrated 'blue water' ops off the coast of San Diego in order to attain full 24-hour deck qualifications for their pilots. After a successful 'at sea' period, the squadron returned to Arizona and began preparing themselves for their forthcoming WestPac deployment aboard *Belleau Wood*'s sister ship, USS *Tarawa* (LHA-1)

Postwar, several Med cruises were completed aboard *Midway* and *Coral Sea* with the venerable Corsair, before a redesignation to VMA-211 in 1952 signalled that the unit was soon to receive a more modern combat type. This arrived in the shape of the AD-2 Skyraider at the end of the year, the early model 'Able Dogs' being replaced by AD-4 and -4B versions in 1954. Following three years of service with the 'Spad', the squadron began its long association with the Skyhawk, (as detailed in chapter one of this volume), on 9 September 1957

**Right** Salt water corrosion is an inherent risk associated with 'blue water' ops, so deckcrews and squadron maintainers strive to keep the levels of sea spray deposits that collect within the airframe down to a minimum by vigorous washing and cleaning at every available opportunity. One routine that is carried out religiously shortly after the engine has spooled-up is the thorough watering of the cavernous intakes, the desalinated liquid being ingested into the turbofan and sprayed out the nozzles after washing the moveable parts during its passage through the powerplant. This routine is also performed shortly after the aircraft has recovered back aboard the carrier, prior to the pilot hitting the engine 'kill' switch and the deck crew 'spotting' the AV-8B(NA)

**Above** Firmly shackled to the carrier's deck by numerous tie-down chains, two virtually brand new AV-8B(NA)s bask in the warm spring sun on the stern of *Belleau Wood*. The '00' and '01' modex numbers on these aircraft signify that, in name at least, these jets belong to the MAG boss and unit commander respectively, although in reality they will be flown by any line pilot. One of the most colourful squadrons in the Corps, VMA-211 were initially activated back in January 1937 as VF-4M. Assigned an assortment of period navy biplanes prior to standardizing on the F3F-1 the following year, the unit was redesignated VMF-2 soon after its formation. Forward deployed to Hawaii in January 1941 as part of MAG-2, VMF-2 was redesignated as VMF-211 five months later and then issued with F4F-3 Wildcats. Soon after its re-equipment with the new Grumman fighter, the unit sent a detachment of aircraft to Wake Island. Days after the infamous Pearl Harbor raid, VMF-211's det fought a bitter defensive action against an overwhelming force of Japanese carrier aircraft, the 'leathernecks' battling on until the island was surrendered on 23 December. Awarded a Presidential Unit Citation for its heroic last stand, VMF-211 continued to wage war against the Japanese across the Pacific right up until the cessation of hostilities in August 1945. Aside from a brief reorganizational period in early 1942 in Hawaii when the squadron was equipped with F2A-3 Buffalos, VMF-211 flew F4F-4 Wildcats and F4U-1/4 Corsairs for the remainder of the 'island-hopping' campaign.

**Above and right** Motioned forward and aligned through hand signals with the thick yellow take-off guide stripe which dissects the deck from stem to stern, the pilot awaits the word from the Launch Officer (LO) to open the throttle, release the brakes and power off down the deck. Known as 'paddles', the LO combines radio communication with recognized hand signals to relay his message to the pilot, who, in true nautical tradition, will salute the LO to indicate that all is well and he is ready to launch. 'Paddles' will watch the ships' motion for pitch and roll, hitting the deck and pointing to the bow just as the vessel begins to rise out of a swell, and thus allowing the aircraft to launch with the carrier in a slightly stem high attitude. Reacting swiftly to his prompting by the LO, the pilot pushes the throttle to MAX and eases off the brakes. As the aircraft passes over the STO line across the bow of the deck, he pulls the nozzle control lever back to the inflight pre-set stop position, which is usually at 50°, and powers away from the carrier

**Above left** Aside from performing their hair-raising acts of 'daring do' at medium to low altitudes with a variety of weapons, and indulging in the occasional ACM 'furball' with other fast jet pilots, the average Harrier II 'jock' must also spend some of his stick time perfecting the more mundane things in life like aerial refuelling. Carrying as much offensive weaponry as a Piper Cub, an AV-8B(NA) is positioned by its pilot immediately astern of a KC-130F from VMGR-352, the tanker having been sent up from its El Toro base specifically for this training cycle. During the mission each VMA-211 jet took it in turns to 'plug in' to the Hercules' wing-tip trailing drogues and take on 1000 lbs (680 US gal) of fuel, the tanking take place at 19,000 ft. Besides the AV-8B(NA)'s distinctive nose fairing (which contains a GEC sensors forward-looking infrared device), the aircraft also boasts an extra pair of cooling ducts sited inboard of the wing leading-edge extensions. The FLIR, coupled with Catseye Night Vision Goggles (NVGS), compatible cockpit lighting and more advanced moving map and head-down displays, make the aircraft a far more accurate strike platform than the day-limited baseline AV-8B. As with the A-4M and the original Harrier II, the AV-8B(NA) still retains the Hughes ASB-19(V)-2 ARBS in the extreme nose section – this venerable system has been deleted to make

room for the Hughes AN/APG-65 radar in the latest AV-8B version, the Harrier II Plus, which is currently undergoing flight testing at McDonnell Douglas

**Above right** With the rugged hills east of Yuma providing a breathtaking backdrop, a tight brace of AV-8B(NA)s close on the lumbering KC-130F prior to splitting up and tanking from the wingtip refuelling pods. Located on either side of the ram air inlet at the base of the fin are a pair of Goodyear/Tracor AN/ALE-39 chaff/flare dispensers, this style of external mounting being unique to the Night Attack variant; a further pair are housed underneath the rear fuselage of the aircraft. The Harrier II's inability to sustain flak and missile damage in the Gulf seriously concerned the Corps, who lost five aircraft in combat. As a result of these shootdowns, the AV-8B fleet is to be fitted with an enhanced version of the AN/APR-44(V) missile approach warning system, as carried by many USMC helicopters. More kinematic chaff/flare dispenser boxes will also be retrofitted to the AV-8B, and the aircraft's internal hydraulic lines hardened (particularly beneath the wing near the exhaust nozzles) to increase their resistance to flak and missile damage

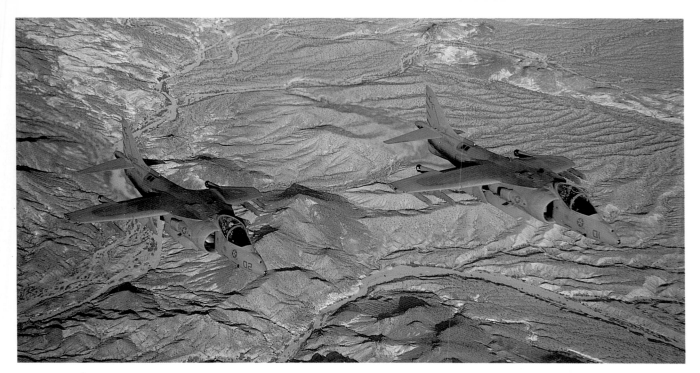

**Below right** Operating standard AV-8Bs alongside VMA-211 at Yuma is VMA-311 'Tomcats', this squadron having deployed to King Abdul Aziz Airfield in 1990 as part of Desert Shield.  Stripped of its wing pylons, bar the two outer stations, and equipped with a dayglo telemetry pod, this heavily exhaust-stained AV-8B pulls on positive G as its pilot rolls into the wispy cloud way above the Yuma weapons range.  Just visible below the fuselage formation lighting strip are the underbelly chaff boxes, the baseline AV-8B originally being fitted with only a pair of these devices in this position. As mentioned earlier, the number of AN/ALE-39 dispensers scabbed onto the Harrier II is to increase to six boxes.  Like several other AV-8B units within MAG-13, VMA-311 transitioned to Harrier IIs fromA-4Ms in 1989 following over 30 years of service to the Corps with their Skyhawks

**Above and right** 'AV-8tor' regalia! The circular patch is worn by many line pilots at Yuma, the rider 'Close Air Support' having been embossed on the finished article to remind the wearer of his purpose in life. The 'double centurion' patches obviously belong to a senior member of VMA-211 – these highly prized items signify the completion of 100 deck landings per patch. By the time VMA-211 completed their 1992/93 WestPac, which lasted six months and took them to the Persian Gulf, Somalia, Australia and the Far East, the squadron had run out of centurion patches

# Multi-mission Hornet

**Right** Heavily involved in patrolling the air exclusion zone over Bosnia with the 6th Fleet for much of 1993, a weaponless F/A-18C from VFA-15 'Valions' enjoys the ride down USS *Theodore Roosevelt*'s (CVN-71) waist catapult during carrier work-ups off Virginia in February 1993. One of the last F/A-18A operators within AirLant, the 'Valions' traded in their Lot IX Hornets for factory-fresh Lot XIV F/A-18Cs soon after successfully completing an extended combat deployment to the Middle East with the remainder of CVW-8 aboard *'TR'*.  VFA-15 and CVN-71 have been inextricably linked since the *Nimitz* class carrier first entered service in 1987, the 'Valions' participating in the vessel's work-ups prior to it joining the Atlantic Fleet.  A veteran of many 6th Fleet cruises over the past five years, *'TR's'* decks have played host to VFA-15 on every single one of those deployments

**Above** Six months prior to *Desert Storm*, VFA-15 flew west to Fallon from their Cecil Field home to meet up with other CVW-8 squadrons and collectively participate in an intensive work-up phase at the 'Strike University'. This exhaustive det followed a short shakedown cruise aboard *'TR'*, which helped prepare the carrier for the air wing's arrival for refresher training (Reftra) in June 1990. Air wings take the Fallon 'get together' very seriously, and squadrons ensure that their jets are in the best possible condition both internally and externally prior to the 17-day work-up; witness the spotless finish on this line F/A-18A, which totes an inert Mk 82R 500 lb bomb (fitted with a BSU-86 retard fin kit) on its port hardpoint. As with many AirLant units, the 'Valions' have a rich history that can be traced back to the months immediately following the disaster at Pearl Harbour. Formed on 10 January 1942 with SBD Dauntlesses as VT-4 aboard USS *Ranger* (CV-4), the squadron first tasted action during the *Torch* landings in North Africa that same year. Avengers replaced the Douglas workhorse in 1943, and the squadron commenced operations in the Pacific whilst assigned to USS *Bunker Hill's* (CV-17) air wing. After the war, the unit was redesignated VA-2A in November 1946, this further changing to VA-15 in August 1948. The following year they moved to Cecil Field and finally replaced their Avengers with AD-4 Skyraiders. A succession of Med cruises with the 6th Fleet kept the unit busy over the next 16 years until VA-15 bade farewell to the 'Spad' in 1965 and received A-4Bs in its place. Two combat tours to Vietnam were completed aboard USS *Intrepid* (CVS-11) in 1966/67, the squadron being heavily involved in *Rolling Thunder* strikes during its spells in the Tonkin Gulf – a total of 2672 combat sorties were flown for the loss of five jets (two pilots were listed as MIA, one was made a POW and the remaining pair were recovered) during the 1967 WestPac. On 1 June 1969 the 'Valions' were disestablished as an A-4 squadron, and the following day VA-67 was renumbered VA-15 and equipped with A-7B Corsair IIs – I'm sure this made sense to someone at AirLant at the time! The Bravo model was replaced by the definitive Echo in October 1975, and the squadron went on to perform annual Med cruises aboard the *America, Nimitz* and *Independence,* before transitioning onto the F/A-18A as VFA-15 in October 1986

**Right** Photographed from the island of USS *Constellation* (CV-64) during the carrier's independent steaming exercise off the Californian coast in April 1988, this VFA-25 'Fist of the Fleet' F/A-18A sits on the deck with its twin GE F404 turbofans idling over on low RPM. As soon as it is his turn to taxy towards a catapult, the pilot will ease his foot off the brake and follow the various signals from deck marshall to deck marshall until he is accurately lined up with his designated launch spot. The Hornet's most distinctive feature, the Leading Edge Extension (LEX), which flanks the spine from the wing to the cockpit, dominates this overhead view. Subtly curved to capture and distribute the airflow most beneficially, the LEX allows the pilot to achieve amazing nose-up angles of attack (AOA) whilst still in full control of the aircraft. Providing the levels of lift necessary to perform such manoeuvres, the device also minimises associated lift and supersonic trim drag, as well as smoothing out AOA buffet. However, because of their thin construction, the LEXs cannot be used for the carriage of fuel as that would destroy the aircraft's trim balance, or the housing of a weapon, because the associated bulging of the device would ruin the smoothly distributed airflow; only the pilot's ladder has found a home in the port LEX so far. The high instantaneous turn rate enjoyed by the Hornet due to its 5.2m$^2$ LEX area is to be further improved in the next generation F/A-18E/F, which will boast a 7m$^2$ area. This device also improves the engine stall margin as it reduces compressor distortion at high AOA

**Above** On a carrier deck each airwing community has its own 'territory' in which to park its aircraft. The fighter squadrons take the stern, the AEWs range in tight alongside the island with the rotary-winged unit, the heavy attackers share space forward of the superstructure and the massed ranks of light strikers assemble on the bow. All equipped with the nose tow bars and wingtip-mounted AIM-9Ms, a uniformly grey swarm of Hornets await the next cycle of ops aboard the *'Connie'* during the 1988 Reftra period at sea. The two most experienced (in terms of time put in) frontline Hornet squadrons currently serving in the Navy, VFAs -25 and -113 transitioned from A-7Es to early-build F/A-18As at Lemoore in 1983. Assigned to CVW-14, the units participated in their first WestPac aboard CV-64 between February and August 1985; both squadrons stayed with this vessel until it went in for a Service Life Extension Period (SLEP) in late 1989. Reassigned with CVW-14 to

the recently refurbished USS *Independence* (CV-62), the squadrons transitioned to Lot XI F/A-18Cs at the same time, their weary Alphas being sent to the North Island NARF before being reissued to various Navy reserve units. Following two highly successful WestPacs aboard *'Indy'*, CVW-14 switched carriers again as CV-62 shifted ports to Yokosuka, Japan, to replace the veteran USS *Midway* (CV-41), which was finally being retired. Besides changing vessels, both VFAs swapped their jets for CVW-5's older Lot VIII F/A-18As, which they duly took back to Lemoore aboard *Midway*. Following several months of flying the old Alphas, the squadrons transitioned to Lot XIV F/A-18Cs in late 1991, these jets boasting both an NVG capability and a ring-base inertial navigation system. Still part of CVW-14, VFAs -25 and -113 now ply their trade from the recently refitted USS *Carl Vinson* (CVN-70)

**Right** Carefully threading his way through the packed flightdeck towards the waist catapults, the pilot of this faded F/A-18A from VFA-113 will lock the folded wingtips of this jet in the down position once he has positioned the Hornet on the catapult. Notoriously short-legged when compared to the tireless 'SLUF', the F/A-18 is rarely seen flying from a carrier without a single centreline or, as in this case, two underwing tanks. The squadron was initially equipped with purpose-built oval section 315 US-gal tanks, which McAir technicians designed to be virtually drag free. The tanks proved susceptible to fatigue after excessive high-G manoeuvring, however, and were replaced by conventional circular ones of 330 US-gal capacity, as worn by this jet

**Above** Fancying himself as a potential 'Blue Angel', VFA-27 'Chargers' XO Cdr Tom 'Smoothdog' Vaughn participated in this rare sortie (flown in July 1991) which put three generations of light strike hardware in the same patch of sky. The Corsair II featured in this photograph was actually an ex-VA-27 aircraft, phased out by the 'Chargers' seven months earlier. Clearly visible in both formation shots is the 'USS Kitty Hawk' titling on the Hornet's twin fins, this marking having been applied whilst the vessel was still in the hands of the shipyard!

**Right** As mentioned in the Corsair II chapter, VFA-27 were the last West Coast squadron within the light strike community to make the switch to the Hornet. Equipped with new F/A-18Cs in January 1991, the 'Chargers' quickly worked through their training cycles on the Hornet, receiving a little help from seasoned campaigners VFA-125 'Rough Raiders' along the way. The squadron's first real at sea test came in October 1991 when, along with other CVW-15 units, they crossed the US to join their 'new' home at Norfolk Naval Yard. *Kitty Hawk* had just finished a four-year long SLEP and was rejoining the Pacific Fleet as a replacement for *Constellation*. For two months the unit flew concentrated 'blue water' ops as the carrier steamed around Cape Horn and back up to San Diego. Two months prior to the deployment, Cdr Vaughn was tasked with flying a sortie that was just a little out of the ordinary for VFA-27; a formation fly-by over Lemoore with an F4U-5 Corsair and an AD-5 Skyraider. Relying on the LEX's lift to keep him in position at piston-engined formation speeds, Vaughn leads the strike package past the main runway threshold at the California base. Lt Col Don Hanna (USMC ret) is at the controls of the Skyraider, and Dick Bertea is doing the honours in the immaculate Corsair

**Above** Perfectly illustrating the multi-role capability of the Hornet, a flight of VFA-87 jets depart Fallon tasked with hitting a mock target out on the live ranges, the aircraft being armed up with a goodly selection of sand-filled Mk 82 500 lb LDGP 'blue bombs'. Relying on their fighter optimised buddies (who had launched immediately prior to the bombed up F/A-18s) to protect them from the 'Cylon' adversaries, each of the strike Hornets nevertheless toted an AIM-9M acquisition round on their wingtip pylons just in case the VFA-127 jocks proved overly persistent – the growl of a locked on Sidewinder quickly focuses the mind of any adversary.

'Fires lit', ailerons and flaps deployed and tailplanes appropriately angled, the CAG of CVW-8 (the aptly named Capt Bill Fallon) gently applies back pressure on the control column whilst keeping the throttle firmly in Burner. The Hornet usually unsticks at about 140 knots depending on its warload, and two 500 pounders and a couple of external tanks are not going to trouble it too much. Sticking to the age old naval tradition of marking the commander air group's aircraft in air wing colours, VFA-87 decorated their 'boss bird' with an appropriately bright chief's head motif

**Below** Two years after their 1990 Fallon det, VFA-87 headed west from Florida to Nevada once again for a full CVW-8 work-up. By this stage fully equipped with state-of-the-art F/A-18Cs, the 'Golden Warriors' flew many pin-point night strike sorties using all manner of ingress and egress techniques during their time at Fallon. Performing the 'day shift' on this occasion, sans NVGs, VFA-87's boss, and his wingman, model the latest in squadron colours high above the range in September 1992. The various spine and nose lumps and bumps associated with the upgraded Sanders EW fit installed in the Charlie model are clearly visible on both jets, as are the extra VHF/IFF/Data Link blade aerials. The EW suite on the F/A-18C consists of the vastly upgraded ITT/Westinghouse AN/ALQ-165 Airborne Self-Protection Jammer (ASPJ), which has replaced the earlier Sanders AN/ALQ-126B system fitted in the earlier F/A-18As. Although the two suites are technically interchangeable, the ASPJ is the favoured system as it can handle a larger array of threats across a wider-frequency band. The extra bulges are in fact about the only external difference between the Alpha and Charlie models, although the story beneath the skin is moderately different

**Right** Firmly attached to waist cat two's shuttle aboard the *'TR'*, 'Warrior 407' is given a quick visual check before the all-clear for launch is signalled. Crouched beneath the aircraft's starboard wing, a launch crew armourer physically shakes the AGM-65F Maverick training round to ensure that the missile is safely attached to the LAU-117 launch rail. Following standard naval deck safety policy, the pilot has clearly raised both hands away from his controls so as to avoid accidentally activating any of the aircraft's systems which could endanger the health of the sailor beneath the Hornet. He will rest his arms on the cockpit sill until instructed through hand signals and across the radio link that the launch crew are satisfied that the F/A-18 is safe for a cat shot. Aside from the Maverick, this aircraft has three external tanks fitted – an unusual configuration rarely seen except when the pilot is performing a long-distance over-water deployment. A relatively youthful squadron when compared with other AirLant light strike units, VA-87 formed on 1 February 1968 specifically to operate the Navy's first A-7Bs. A single war cruise to South-east Asia aboard USS *Ticonderoga* (CVS-14) was performed just over a year later, the squadron then establishing a routine pattern of 6th Fleet deployments throughout the 1970s; *Franklin D Roosevelt*, *America* and *Independence* all played host to VA-87 between 1971 and 1979. The squadron was also periodically involved in various operations in the Middle East, ranging from monitoring the Arab-Israeli conflict, through to covering the evacuation of citizens from the Lebanon in 1976 whilst part of *America*'s air wing. The squadron also participated in the Indian Ocean vigil maintained by the Navy during the Iranian hostage crisis of 1980/81 aboard *Independence,* and then the following year re-aquainted itself with the Lebanese coast as the squadron was tasked with supporting US peacekeeping forces in the beleaguered country. Twelve months later, the 'Golden Warriors' were involved yet  again in an historic *'Indy'*cruise, VA-87 flying strike missions in two separate conflicts – over Grenada in support of the island invasion by the US Army's 82nd Airborne and Rangers divisions, and against Syrian artillery and radar sites in the Lebanese hills. Following a long and chequered history with the Corsair II, the Golden Warriors were redesignated VFA-87 on 1 May 1986 and issued with F/A-18As soon after

**Above** It takes between six and eight months to turn a 'nugget' pilot fresh from basic flying training school into a fully fledged fleet naval aviator totally checked out in a frontline type, each community having its own Fleet Replacement Squadron (FRS) dedicated to honing the raw skill of an inexperienced ensign or lieutenant (junior grade). Formerly an A-4 Skyhawk RAG (Replacement Air Group) that then transitioned onto the A-7A/B in 1969, VFA-125 became the first F/A-18 squadron in the Navy on 13 November 1980 when it reactivated three years after retiring its last Corsair IIs. VFA-125's first Hornet arrived at Lemoore on 19 February 1981, and the unit's primary task was to train up its own instructor pilots and groundcrews; an initial batch of 16 Navy and Marine pilots from both strike and fighter backgrounds were checked out on the aircraft using an embryonic training syllabus which has since been honed and refined over the ensuing decade. The final stage of the work-up saw the crews take the aircraft to sea for a week of solid carquals, the first such deployment taking place between 27 September and 4 October 1982 when six pilots from VFA-127 successfully completed an intensive day and night training period aboard *Constellation*. A decade later, VFA-125 was photographed at sea once again, yet another class of aspiring naval aviators nearing the end of their two-and-half-years of training, the culmination of which is two weeks of intensive 'blue water' ops aboard a frontline fleet carrier. Having just arrived on board following a short flight out from Lemoore, ace instructor Cdr Chris 'Nutts' Nutter is guided towards his 'spot' in front of USS *Nimitz*'s (CVN-68) island structure

**Above right** With very little room left for error, the pilot of BuNo 164050 places his life squarely in the hands of the experienced deck marshaller who is guiding him with hand signals towards the carrier's round-down. Just when it appears that the Hornet has gone too far down the deck and the pilot would perhaps benefit from pulling down tautly on his ejection handles, the marshaller will signal for a sharp turn to port and the F/A-18 will eventually come to rest exactly where the air boss wants it. The engines will be shut down and the clutch of sailors to the left of the Hornet will surge forward and secure the aircraft to the deck using tie-down chairs and wheel chocks. Although the carrier has been cleared of its frontline air wing prior to the FRS deployment, the vessel's deck crew marshal the 'nugget' pilots around Nimitz's 'roof' as if a full complement of 90+ aircraft were embarked, thus increasing the realism and value of the training on offer

**Below right** The positioning of the Hornet's built-in M61A1 20 mm Vulcan cannon was dictated by the lack of space either in the wing LEX or between the nosegear well and the AN/APG-65's avionics equipment-bay. Lying literally above the radar, and its associated 'black boxes', the compact gatling gun has failed to cause the problems to the operability of the sophisticated Hughes avionics that many predicted it would. A further bonus enjoyed by the F/A-18 due to the gun's positioning is that the gases produced when firing the weapon are easily diverted away from the engine intakes by a fixed deflector, which splits the blast and channels it out over the LEXs, thus eliminating any possibility of a stall. Sandwiched between the radar equipment module and the cockpit bulkhead is the 570-round ammunition drum and linkless feed chute

**Above and right** Although initially equipped with a large fleet of F/A-18A/Bs, VFA-125 realigned itself with future fleet needs in the late 1980s when it began receiving the first F/A-18C/Ds issued to AirPac direct from McAir at St Louis. Just beginning to exhibit the tell-tale engine stains associated with every day fleet use beneath their rear fuselages, these two near-new airframes were photographed on a training hop out of Lemoore in September 1991, six months after their entry in service. Leading 'Raider 64' flight in modex 550 is Lt Col 'Altas' Kennedy, his wingman on this occasion being student pilot Capt 'Squeeze' Damm. Formed to train both Marine Corps and Navy air- and groundcrews, VFA-125 was solely responsible for this task up until the re-equipment of VMFAT-101 'Sharpshooters' at El Toro in October 1987. Equipped with F/A-18A/Bs, the latter unit currently sends crews destined for Charlie or Delta model Hornets to VFA-125 for conversion training. Both jets carry what appear to be AAW-7 airborne armament remote control datalink pods for the Walleye guided missile on single underwing hardpoints

**Above** Compared with its single-engined predecessor, the F/A-18 is a dream to handle on the approach to a carrier, its ultra-responsive F404s permitting the pilot to rapidly dig himself out of any potentially watery 'hole' he may have drifted into. Combined with the mass of 'wetted' flying surfaces (leading edge slats and trailing edge drooping ailerons) clearly visible in this photograph, the Hornet's 'around the boat' handling characteristics have made it one of the safest aircraft ever sent to sea with the US Navy. An early sign of this was VFA-125's amazing 30,000 accident free hours milestone that it achieved in March 1985 following four years of exhaustive flying with the type – the unit averages 1500 flight hours a month, training up to five classes at once. Nicknamed the 'Rough Raiders', the then VA-125 formed as a Replacement Air Group (RAG) unit equipped with F9F Cougars at NAS Moffett Field, California, on 11 April 1958. The veteran Grumman fighters were soon supplanted by A4D-2s (A-4Bs) two months later as the squadron commenced its Skyhawk conversion tasking. Transferred to the new home of AirPac light strike at NAS Lemoore in July 1961, the unit proceeded to fly all Navy models of the A-4 over the next eight years, providing the fleet with over 2000 pilots and 12,000 maintainers during the same period. In 1966 fellow RAG squadron VA-122 transitioned onto the A-7 Corsair II, and in September 1969 VA-125 followed suit; the unit was issued with the 'Flying Eagles'' Alpha and Bravo model airframes, whilst the latter re-equipped exclusively with A-7Es. Issued in the early 1970s with a number of A-7Cs as well, VA-125 continued to satisfy AirPac's training needs until the light strike community finally phased out their remaining early-model Corsair IIs in 1977. Its job over for the time being, VA-125 disestablished on 1 October 1977, remaining dormant until their reformation as the inaugural F/A-18 FRS three years later

**Below** McAir products from different generations exchange pleasantries prior to indulging in a spot of one v one dissimilar air combat out over the Gulf of Mexico. 'Phantom Phlyers' for 22 years, VMFA-251 'Thunderbolts' transitioned from F-4Ss to F/A-18As at MCAS Beaufort in the spring of 1986, thus becoming only the third Hornet operator within MAG-31 in the process. Twenty years its senior, the Europe One camouflaged F-4D hailed from the 111th Fighter Interceptor Squadron (FIS) at Ellington Air National Guard Station in Houston, the squadron being part of the 'National Air Force of Texas'. When this photograph was taken in August 1989, the 111th FIS was only weeks away from beginning its conversion training onto F-16A/Bs

**Above** In 1985 two Marine Hornet units (VMFAs -314 and -323) participated in an AirLant 6th Fleet cruise aboard *Coral Sea* whilst the Navy's light strike community transitioned a sufficient number of A-7 squadrons over to the F/A-18. By 1986, the shortfall in Navy Hornet units had been rectified, and the Corps' traditionally land-based squadrons returned to their respective MAGs. Three years later, VMFA-451 joined CV-43 for its final Med cruise prior to the carrier's decommissioning in place of VFA-131, who had been temporarily assigned to *Independence*. This random pattern of sea time allocated to USMC Hornet units typified the approach taken by the CNO to Marine Aviation over the decades, the 'flying leathernecks' usually being called on to step into the breach when a frontline Navy unit was either transitioning onto a new type of aircraft, or an air wing needed bolstering for a specific tasking. However, in 1992 this all changed as Rear Admiral Riley Mixson, director of naval aviation, instigated the first steps in a radical overhaul of the traditional air wing configuration. Faced with a drastically reduced budget, Mixson has decided to trim the size of an embarked CVW's offensive strike force from 60 to 50 aircraft, but at the same time making the wing more capable of fulfilling multi-mission taskings. The ideal air wing 'all rounder' is the F/A-18, and realising that congress will not fund the establishment of new Hornet squadrons, the admiral has turned to the Marines yet again to make up the shortfall, although on this occasion the Corps' role is a far more permanent one. An immediate sign of the new composite structure evolving was the allocation of three Hornet squadrons to the Navy, this trio due to be followed by another pair who will alternately perform fleet deployments between traditional MAG taskings. One of the first units affected by Mixson's directives was VMFA-312 'Checkerboards', the youngest of MAG-31's five (originally six – VMFA-333 was disestablished on 31 March 1992) Hornet squadrons being assigned to CVW-8 aboard *Theodore Roosevelt*. Chosen primarily because they were the only Corps' strike unit at that time equipped with fleet-compatible

F/A-18Cs, VMFA-312 began the exhaustive path to 'blue water' ops by joining the air wing for their weapons det to the 'Strike U' at Fallon in September 1992. Distinctively marked with their full-colour twin fin 'checkers' and unusually high modex numbers, VMFA-312 had by this stage 'got with the programme' and exchanged their familiar 'DR' tail codes for CVW-8's 'AJ'. Toting no less than five Mk 82SE Snakeye 500-lb live bombs on various hardpoints (including, rather unusually, the number three centreline station), 'Checker 337' rapidly rolls along one of Fallon's many taxyways out to the runway

**Above** By February 1993 VMFA-312 was putting all of its training into practice as CVW-8 completed a brief refresher exercise in the Atlantic for the benefit of both the air wing and *'TR'* itself. Although most of the flying was completed sans external weaponry, the Hornets were flown with typical at sea drop tank fitments, however, ranging from a single centreline store to three tanks, as carried by this aircraft. Despite the powerful kick of the cat shot, the aircraft's impressive lift devices and full afterburning thrust of two F404-GE-400 turbofans (rated at 16,000 lbs each), the heavily laden Hornet still sinks slightly as the deck of the carrier runs out. Aside from the 330 US gal tanks, this aircraft also boasts a Ford AN/AAS-38 FLIR pod nestled into the starboard missile trough. Joining VMFA-312 aboard *'TR'* was a 600-man Special Purpose Marine Air-Ground Task Force (MAGTF), equipped with six CH-53Ds and four UH-1Ns, as well as associated ground assault equipment. Configured for non-combatant evacuation, security support for larger operations, combat raids, humanitarian and disaster assistance and SAR work, the MAGTF was a further illustration of the broadening of the air wing's future mission tasking. To make space for the Corps', a squadron of Tomcats and a squadron of Intruders were left ashore at Oceana – Mixson eventually wants to retire all A-6s from frontline service by 1999, the venerable bomber being replaced by the F/A-18E/F in the short term

**Above** Looking good for a three-wire/OK grade landing, a silhouetted F/A-18C returns to *'TR'* with its triple ejector rack devoid of Mk 76 bombs. Following the successful completion of the CVW-8/MAGTF work-ups aboard CVN-71, the vessel sailed east for the Med, eventually relieving *John F Kennedy* and taking up station off the former Yugoslavia in order to help the UN enforce the air exclusion zone set up over Bosnia. Boasting a history far older than many current Navy light strike units, the 'Checkerboards' can trace their roots back to June 1943 when VMF-312 was commissioned to fly F4U Corsairs initially from island bases and then from carriers, as the allied forces took the fight to the Japanese in the Pacific. Called to arms once again in 1950, VMF-312 won further honours whilst still equipped with the Corsair over Korea during no less than five Task Force 77 cruises. Twelve years later the 'Checkerboards' were embroiled in conflict yet again, the unit deploying its F-8Es to Da Nang in December 1965. Following the briefest of stays (barely two months!), they returned to Cherry Point and commenced transitioning onto the F-4B. Over the next two decades the squadron participated in a variety of MAG deployments and exercises, including the six-monthly rotational det to WestPac. F-4Js arrived in February 1973, which were in turn replaced by F-4Ss a decade later. The last Phantom II to leave VMFA-312 following the unit's transition onto the F/A-18A departed Beaufort for Davis-Monthan on 29 July 1987

**Above** As VMFA-312 was preparing for its inaugural AirLant cruise, fellow Hornet operators VMFA-314 'Black Knights' were also familiarizing themselves with carrier ops following a six-year hiatus. The first unit in the Marines/Navy to achieve operational status on the Hornet, the 'Black Knights' have been flying F/A-18As since 7 January 1983 (although pilot conversion commenced at VFA-125 five months before). Now part of CVW-11 aboard *Abraham Lincoln*, VMFA-314 have replaced VF-114 'Aardvarks' within the air wing, the latter squadron disbanding on 30 April 1993. Currently still equipped with Alpha model Hornets, the 'Black Knights' have been tasked with performing some of the fighter duties in conjunction with VF-114's former sister-squadron, VF-213 'Black Lions', whilst the F/A-18C-equipped VFAs -22 and -94 carry out the bulk of the light strike missions for CVW-11. Photographed in mid-tank whilst 'spotted' alongside *Nimitz*'s island during CarQuals in June 1992, this weary warrior still carries its *Desert Storm* scoreboard below the starboard LEX and traditional MAG-11 'VW' tail codes on its twin fins. By the time the unit embarked aboard its future home two months later for a further week of CarQuals, VMFA-314 had swapped its 'VW' for a more appropriate 'NH', and modified its two-digit modex into a three-digit number, assuming VF-213's old 200 series range. The 'Black Lions', meanwhile, had adopted VF-114's highly prized 100 series for their F-14As

**Above** When VMFA-314 went to sea with CVW-11, they took their experienced armourers with them. However, due to a severe lack of deck space, the unit was forced to leave its nifty MJ-1 'jammers' behind; the 'loadies' had to physically hump bombs across the roof of CVN-72 from the carrier's lifts to the awaiting squadron aircraft just like their Navy brethren. When this photograph was taken at El Toro in November 1991, Mixson's multi-role air wing directive was but a twinkling in the admiral's eye, VMFA-314 still basking a little in its post-*Desert Storm* glory. Dropping a massive amount of ordnance on a variety of Iraqi targets, VMFA-314 flew a countless number of sorties from the huge USMC facility at Sheikh Isa Air Base in Bahrain. During an anti-tank mission by the squadron one of their aircraft actually had an engine knocked out by a shoulder-launched SA-7 or SA-14 SAM, although the remaining powerplant (itself badly damaged) kept going long enough for the pilot to bring his jet safely home. This combat veteran is being loaded up with inert Mk 82 LDGP bombs, one per ordnance station. The rectangle of fresh paint beneath the cockpit denotes that this aircraft has recently 'changed hands', its pilot during *Desert Storm* having obviously been transferred to another unit since the squadron's return to El Toro

**Below** Toting something a little more lethal than a jousting staff, 'Black Knight 06' sits quietly beneath the moon on a deserted El Toro ramp. The Texas Instruments Paveway laser guidance nose, as fitted to a Mk 82 iron bomb, dominates this view of the aircraft, the combined weapon being designated a GBU-12A Paveway I long wing in USMC parlance. The smallest in terms of bomb weight of the encyclopaedic range of LGBs, this device will nevertheless knock out a T-72 tank with relative ease if the target is 'painted' correctly by a laser designator.

Mounted on station two alongside the Paveway is an AGM-88 HARM (High-Speed Anti-Radiation Missile), this particular weapon having been used by the squadron in the Libyan air strikes during Operations *Prairie Fire* and *Eldorado Canyon* in March/April 1986, and the Gulf War of 1991. Both these devices are inert training rounds, although they still boast active seeker heads so as to allow the pilot to interface his ordnance with the aircraft's sophisticated weapons delivery avionics

**Above** Framing 'Black Knight 06' with its slender nose contours, sister-ship '05' also boasts the familiar VMFA-314 scoreboard. The silhouettes within this distinctive marking symbolise a captured Kuwaiti patrol boat, pressed into service by the Iraqis and duly despatched to the bottom of the Persian Gulf by VMFA-314; a T-72 tank; a FROG-7 missile launcher; a self-propelled gun; and finally a BMP-1 light armoured vehicle. Unlike other Marine tally boards, these symbols have no individual totals denoting how many tanks, guns or FROGs each aircraft destroyed, the marking serving as a unit-wide decoration attributing VMFA-314's success evenly across all of its Hornets, and associated pilots. The panel left ajar immediately above the gun gas purging vents covers the pressurised ground refuelling receptacle, and its associated switchology. A close look at the stencilling beneath the windscreen of this jet reveals that the name of its former 'owner' has been removed

**Right** Just as Marines go to war in fatigues, Marine marshallers direct 'traffic' back at base in exactly the same garb, minus combat webbing, helmet and M-16 assault rifle! Most air station taxyways are liberally adorned with track stripes and undercarriage alignment lines so as to allow the pilot to safely manoeuvre his aircraft across the tarmac to and from the squadron dispersal

**Right** When VMFA-314 packed up
its bags and went east to Norfolk,
Virginia, in preparation for *Coral
Sea*'s impending 6th Fleet cruise, the
'Black Knights' took their MAG-11
buddies VMFA-323 'Death Rattlers'
along with them. In fact, the latter
unit had joined forces with CV-43
once before, the squadron
embarking their F-4Ns aboard the
carrier for its 1979/80 WestPac
deployment. Transitioning to F/A-
18As soon after VMFA-314, the
'Death Rattlers' were re-declared to
MAG-11 in late 1983; following its
highly successful one-off Med
cruise, the unit participated in the
huge *Bright Star* exercise in Egypt in
1987 and performed a six-month
tour of duty forward deployed to
Iwakuni the following year. This
pristine aircraft was photographed
in September 1989 during a
squadron det to Portland
International Airport for a week of
air combat training with the
incumbent 123rd FIS, and their F-4C
Phantom IIs – like most other
Marine Hornet units, VMFA-323
flew F-4s for almost two decades
prior to transitioning onto the
F/A-18

**Above right** Wearing the familiar
skull motif on their twin fins, a
quartet of F/A-18As from
VMFA-531 'Grey Ghosts' idle on the
Hill AFB transient ramp on 4 May
1987, awaiting permission to taxy

out and commence their next dissimilar air combat sorties with the local
F-16 wing, the 388th TFW. To aid in the scoring of the up-coming battle, each
of the Hornets boast a Kelvin ACMI pod on the starboard wingtip launch rail.
Although the Marine aircrews are trained primarily in the art of close air
support 'mud moving' in conjunction with their beach storming brethren on
the ground, any opportunity to practice the 'F' portion of 'F/A-18' is rapidly
exploited; the long cross-country flight from California to Utah and back is
but a small price to pay for ACM training against the best dogfighter in the
business. Single-seat Hornet squadrons often deploy for short periods of time
to both frontline and guard bases to help the incumbent units hone their skills
in the art of dissimilar combat – with the deactivation of the dedicated USAF
aggressor squadrons several years ago, the Corps have been literally
swamped with invitations of ACM from units across America

**Below right** VMFA-531 was the third, and last, MAG-11 F-4N unit to
transition onto the Hornet, the squadron standing up with the F/A-18A in the
summer of 1983. Still equipped with the same early-build airframes four
years later, the squadron jets were beginning to look a little second-hand in
the markings department by this stage – check out the scuffed and seriously
faded overwing walkway. Traces of soot around the muzzle port also denote
that Maj Goodman has indulged in a spot of gunnery practice out over the
Hill AFB live-fire range during his det to the Utah base

**Above** Engines shut down and wheels chocked, Maj Thomas 'de-planes' following an exhaustive ACM 'furball' with his hosts from the 388th TFW. The cause of much of the scuffing on the LEXs and around the cockpit sills is revealed in this photograph – size 10, standard issue, USMC boots. Some of the more image-conscious squadrons within MAG-11 force their air- and groundcrews to don protective slipper covers over their rubber-soled boots prior to climbing all over the aircraft. The TPS has always suffered badly at the hands (or feet) of groundcrew, the rough finish of the paint absorbing much of the grime picked up in the tread of the boots from the flightline

**Left** Configured with ACM in mind, two 'Grey Ghosts' rotate away from Hill, carrying only a centreline tank each and a wingtip AIM-9M acquisition round a piece. Having come through the Gulf War unscathed, VMFA-531 fell victim to budget cuts barely 12 months later, the unit holding its disestablishment ceremony on 31 March 1992. Formed as a dedicated night fighter squadron almost 50 years before, VMF(N)-531 stood up at Cherry Point on 16 November 1942 and entered combat in the South Pacific, equipped with F6F-3N Hellcats, the following September. The squadron won further battle honours over Korea in the 1950s when it flew the portly F3D-2 Skynight on anti-'Bed-check Charlie' missions against North Korean and Chinese nocturnal raiders. Redesignated VMF(AW)-531 in the late 1950s, the unit swapped its Skynights for Skyrays and became one of the few Marine squadrons to fly the all-weather Douglas 'Ford' in the process. In 1962 the 'Grey Ghosts' became the first Corps unit on the East Coast to transition onto the Phantom II, and three years later they deployed to Da Nang, in Vietnam, for a brief two-month tour of duty. The unit received F-4Ns in the summer of 1975, and continued to operate the November model until acquiring its first Hornets in May 1983

# McDonnell Douglas/British Aerospace AV-8B Harrier II

1 Starboard all-moving tailplane
2 Tailplane composite multi-spar construction
3 Tail navigation light
4 Rear radar warning antennae
5 Tail pitch control air valve
6 Yaw control air valves
7 Tail 'bullet' fairing
8 Reaction control system air ducting
9 Trim tab actuator
10 Rudder trim tab
11 Rudder composite construction
12 Rudder
13 Fin-tip antenna
14 Glassfibre aerial facing
15 Upper broad-band communications aerial
16 Port tailplane
17 Graphite epoxy tailplane skin
18 Port side temperature probe
19 MAD compensator
20 Electro-luminescent formation lighting strip
21 Fin construction
22 Fin spar attachment joint
23 Tailplane pivot sealing plate
24 Tailplane attachment double frame
25 Ventral fin
26 Tail bumper
27 Lower broad-band communications aerial
28 Tailplane hydraulic actuator
29 Heat exchanger air exhaust
30 Aft fuselage frames
31 Rudder hydraulic actuator
32 Avionics equipment air conditioning plant
33 Reaction control air ducting
34 Avionics cooling air duct
35 Electrical system circuit breaker panels, port and starboard
36 Battery
37 Heat exchanger ram air intake
38 Fuselage frame and stringer construction
39 Avionics equipment racks
40 Avionics bay access door, port and starboard
41 Electro-luminescent formation lighting strip
42 Ventral airbrake, open
43 Airbrake hydraulic jack
44 Main undercarriage wheel bay
45 Wing root trailing edge fillet
46 Wing spar/fuselage attachment
47 Rear fuselage fuel tanks Total internal capacity 4163 l (1100 US gal)
48 Water filler cap
49 Engine fire-extinguisher bottle
50 Anti-collision light
51 Water tank

52 Flap hydraulic actuator
53 Flap hinge fitting
54 Nimonic fuselage heat shield
55 Main undercarriage bay doors (closed after cycling of mainwheels)
56 Flap vane composite construction
57 Flap composite construction
58 Starboard slotted flap, lowered
59 Outrigger wheel fairing
60 Outrigger leg doors
61 Starboard aileron
62 Fuel tank tail fins
63 Aileron composite construction
64 Fuel jettison
65 Electro-luminescent wing-tip formation light
66 Roll control air valve
67 Wing-tip fairing
68 Starboard navigation light
69 Radar warning antenna
70 AIM-9L Sidewinder air-to-air missile
71 LAU-61 rocket launcher (19 FFAR)
72 LAU-10 rocket launcher (7 FFAR)
73 60 mm Folding Fin Aircraft Rocket (FFAR)
74 Missile launch rail
75 Outboard pylon

76 Pylon attachment joint
77 Graphite epoxy composite wing construction
78 Aileron hydraulic actuator
79 Starboard outrigger wheel
80 External fuel tank, capacity 1135 l (300 US gal)
81 Intermediate pylon
82 Reaction control air ducting
83 Aileron control rod
84 Outrigger hydraulic retraction jack
85 Outrigger leg strut
86 Leg pivot fixing
87 Multi-spar wing construction
88 Leading edge wing fence
89 Inboard pylon
90 Triple ejector rack
91 Snakeye retarded bombs
92 Aft retracting twin mainwheels
93 Inboard pylon attachment joint
94 Rear (hot stream) swivelling exhaust nozzle
95 Position of pressure refuelling connection on port side
96 Rear nozzle bearing
97 Centre fuselage flank fuel tank
98 Hydraulic reservoir
99 Nozzle bearing cooling air duct
100 Engine exhaust divider duct
101 Wing panel centre rib
102 Centre section integral fuel tank
103 Port wing integral fuel tank
104 Flap vane
105 Port slotted flap, lowered

106 Outrigger wheel fairing
107 Port outrigger wheel
108 Torque scissor links
109 Port aileron
110 Aileron hydraulic actuator
111 Aileron/air valve interconnection
112 Fuel jettison
113 Electro-luminescent wing-tip formation light
114 Port roll control air valve
115 Port navigation light
116 Radar warning antenna
117 TAV-8B two-seat training variant
118 Increased area tail fin
119 Instructor's cockpit enclosure
120 Student pilot's cockpit enclosure
121 Rockeye II cluster bomb
122 Port outboard pylon
123 Port wing reaction control air duct
124 Fuel pumps
125 Fuel system piping

126 Port wing leading-edge fence
127 Intermediate pylon
128 Port external fuel tank
129 Paveway II (GBU-16) laser-guided bomb
130 General Electric GAU 12/U five-barrel, 25 mm rotary cannon (port gun pack fairing only)
131 Port leading-edge root extension (LERX)
132 Inboard stores pylon
133 Hydraulic pumps
134 APU intake
135 Gas turbine starter/auxiliary power unit (APU)

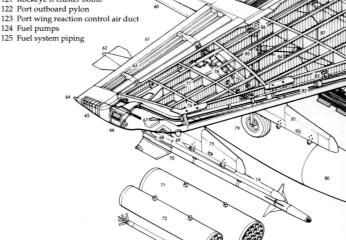

136 Alternator cooling air exhaust
137 APU exhaust
138 Engine fuel control unit
139 Engine bay venting ram air intake
140 Rotary nozzle bearing
141 Nozzle fairing construction
142 Ammunition feed chute
143 Fuel vent
144 Starboard gun pack
    fairing/ammunition magazine
145 Ventral strake

146 Zero-scarf forward (fan air) swivelling
    nozzle
147 Fuselage centreline pylon
148 Mk 83 447 kg (985 lb) HE bomb
149 AGM-65A Maverick laser-guided air-
    to-surface missile
150 Ammunition magazine, 300 rounds
151 Engine drain mast
152 Hydraulic system ground connections
153 Forward fuselage tank
154 Engine electronic control units
155 Engine accessory equipment gearbox
156 Gearbox-driven alternator
157 Rolls-Royce Pegasus F402-RR-406
    vectored thrust turbofan engine
158 Electro-luminescent formation lighting
    strips

159 Engine oil tank
160 Bleed air spill duct
161 Air conditioning intake scoop
162 Cockpit air conditioning system heat
    exchanger
163 Engine compressor/fan face
164 Heat exchanger discharge to intake
    duct
165 Nose undercarriage hydraulic
    retraction jack
166 Intake blow-in doors
167 Engine bay venting air scoop
168 Ammunition pack nose fairing
169 Lift augmentation retractable
    cross-dam
170 Cross-dam hydraulic jack
171 Nosewheel, forward retracting
172 Nosewheel forks
173 Landing/taxiing lamp
174 Retractable boarding step

175 Nosewheel doors (closed after cycling
    of undercarriage)
176 Nosewheel door jack
177 Boundary layer bleed air duct
178 Nose undercarriage wheel bay
179 Kick-in boarding steps
180 Cockpit rear pressure bulkhead
181 Starboard side console panel
182 Stencil 'zero-zero' ejection seat
183 Safety harness
184 Ejection seat headrest
185 Port engine air intake
186 Probe hydraulic jack
187 Retractable in-flight refuelling probe
    (bolt-on pack)
188 Cockpit canopy cover
189 Miniature detonating cord (MDC)
    canopy breaker
190 Canopy frame
191 Engine throttle and nozzle angle
    control levers
192 Pilot's head-up display
193 Instrument panel
194 Moving map display
195 Control column
196 Central warning system panel
197 Cockpit pressure floor
198 Underfloor control runs
199 Electro-luminescent formation
    lighting strips
200 Aileron trim actuator
201 Rudder pedals
202 Cockpit section composite
    construction
203 Instrument panel shroud
204 One-piece wrap-around
    windscreen panel
205 Ram air intake (cockpit fresh air)
206 Front pressure bulkhead
207 Incidence vane
208 Air data computer
209 Pitot tube
210 Lower IFF aerial
211 Nose pitch control air valve
212 Pitch trim control actuator
213 Electrical system equipment
214 Yaw vane
215 Upper IFF aerial
216 Weapons system equipment
217 ARBS heat exchanger
218 Hughes Angle Rate Bombing Set
    (ARBS)
219 Composite construction nose cone
220 ARBS television/laser seeker/tracker
    glazed aperture

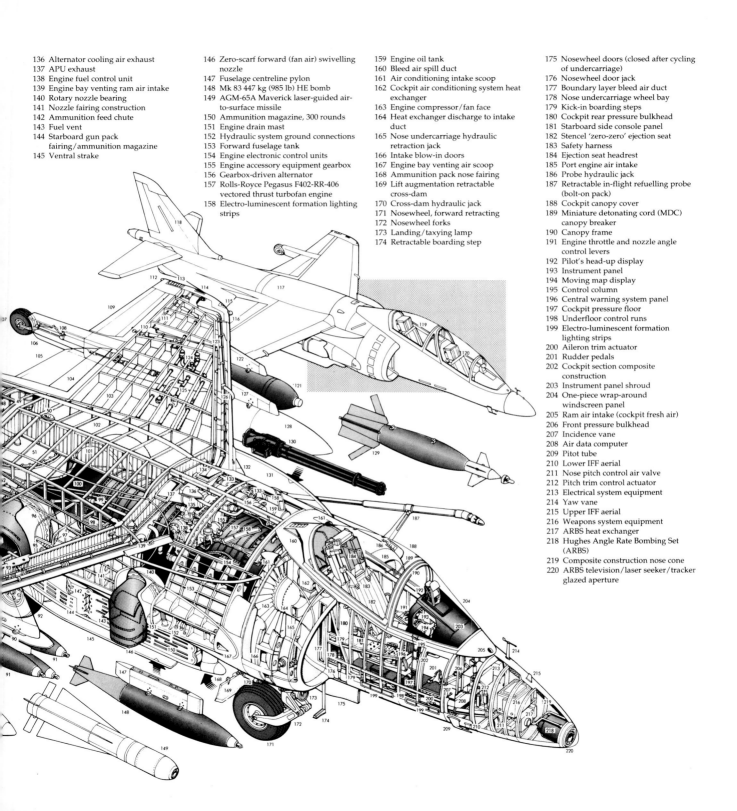

# McDonnell Douglas A-4M Skyhawk

1 Fixed inflight-refuelling probe
2 Nose ECM recording and suppression aerials
3 Angle Rate Bombing System (ARBS) laser seeker head
4 Hinged nose compartment access door
5 Laser seeker system electronics
6 Electronics cooling air inlet
7 Pitot tube
8 Avionics access panel
9 APN-153(V) navigation radar
10 Lower TACAN aerial
11 Communications electronics
12 Cockpit front pressure bulkhead
13 Pressurization valve
14 Windshield rain dispersal air duct
15 Rudder pedals
16 Angle-of-attack sensor
17 Air conditioning refrigeration plant
18 Nosewheel door
19 Control system access
20 Cockpit floor level
21 Pilot's side console panel
22 Engine throttle
23 Control column
24 Instrument panel shroud
25 Head-up display (HUD)
26 Windscreen panels
27 AIM-9L Sidewinder air-to-air missile
28 Missile launch rail
29 D-704 flight refuelling pack containing 300 US gal (1135 l)
30 Cockpit canopy cover
31 Face blind firing handle
32 Ejection seat headrest
33 Safety harness
34 McDonnell Douglas Escapac 1-G3 'zero-zero' ejection seat
35 Anti-g valve
36 Cockpit insulation and fragmentation blanket
37 Rear pressure bulkhead
38 Emergency canopy release handle
39 Nose undercarriage leg strut
40 Steering linkage
41 Nosewheel
42 Leg shortening link
43 Hydraulic retraction strut
44 Emergency wind-driven generator
45 Port cannon muzzle
46 Intake gun gas shield
47 Port air intake
48 Boundary layer splitter plate
49 Self-sealing fuselage fuel cell, capacity 240 US gal (908 l)
50 Fuel system piping
51 Canopy hinge cover
52 Starboard air intake duct
53 Fuel system gravity filler cap
54 UHF aerial
55 Electronics cooling air inlet
56 Engine-driven generator

57 Constant-speed drive unit
58 Bifurcated intake duct
59 Reel type ammunition magazine (200 rounds per gun)
60 Intake compressor face
61 Electrical system power amplifier
62 Engine accessory drive gearbox
63 Wing spar attachment fuselage double frame
64 Engine mounting trunion
65 Engine fuel system access panel
66 Pratt & Whitney J52-P-408 turbojet
67 Dorsal avionics bays
68 Compressor bleed air exhaust duct
69 Upper TACAN aerial

70 Starboard wing integral fuel tank (total wing tank capacity 560 US gal/2120 l)
71 Wing tank access panels
72 Slat guide rails
73 Starboard automatic leading-edge slat (open)
74 Wing fences
75 Vortex generators
76 Starboard navigation light
77 Wing tip communications aerial
78 Aileron horn balance
79 Starboard aileron
80 Split trailing-edge flap
81 Split trailing-edge flap (down position)
82 Anti-collision light
83 Cooling air exit louvres

84 Rear fuselage double frame break point
85 Engine firewall
86 Cooling air intake
87 VHF aerial
88 Upper fuselage stringers
89 Fin root dorsal fairing
90 Remote compass flux valve
91 Rear electronics bay cooling air inlet
92 Fin rib construction
93 Fin spar attachment joint
94 Rudder hydraulic jack
95 Artificial feel spring unit
96 Pitot tube

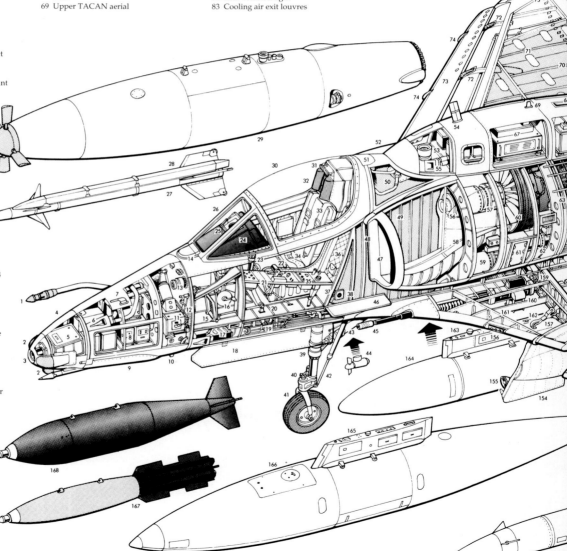

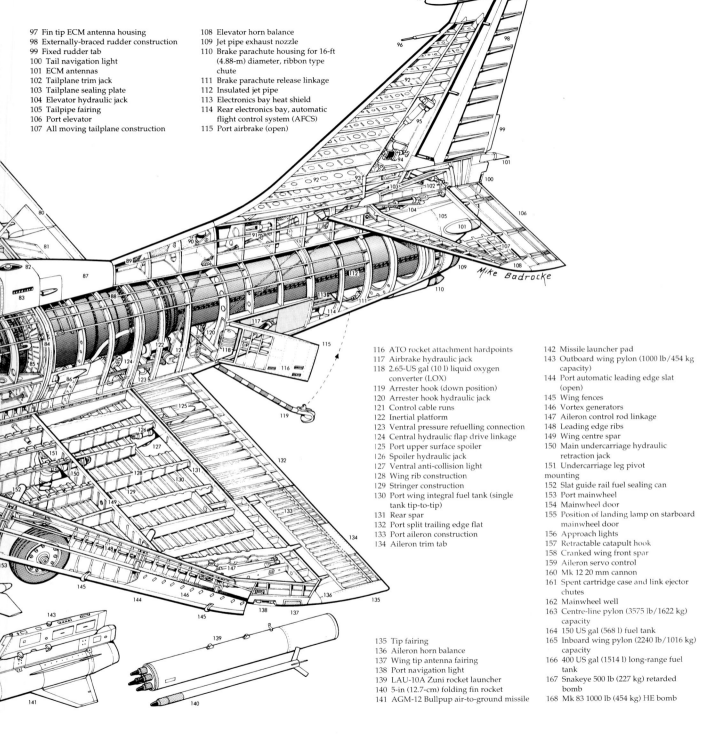

97 Fin tip ECM antenna housing
98 Externally-braced rudder construction
99 Fixed rudder tab
100 Tail navigation light
101 ECM antennas
102 Tailplane trim jack
103 Tailplane sealing plate
104 Elevator hydraulic jack
105 Tailpipe fairing
106 Port elevator
107 All moving tailplane construction

108 Elevator horn balance
109 Jet pipe exhaust nozzle
110 Brake parachute housing for 16-ft
    (4.88-m) diameter, ribbon type
    chute
111 Brake parachute release linkage
112 Insulated jet pipe
113 Electronics bay heat shield
114 Rear electronics bay, automatic
    flight control system (AFCS)
115 Port airbrake (open)

Mike Badrocke

116 ATO rocket attachment hardpoints
117 Airbrake hydraulic jack
118 2.65-US gal (10 l) liquid oxygen
    converter (LOX)
119 Arrester hook (down position)
120 Arrester hook hydraulic jack
121 Control cable runs
122 Inertial platform
123 Ventral pressure refuelling connection
124 Central hydraulic flap drive linkage
125 Port upper surface spoiler
126 Spoiler hydraulic jack
127 Ventral anti-collision light
128 Wing rib construction
129 Stringer construction
130 Port wing integral fuel tank (single
    tank tip-to-tip)
131 Rear spar
132 Port split trailing edge flat
133 Port aileron construction
134 Aileron trim tab

142 Missile launcher pad
143 Outboard wing pylon (1000 lb/454 kg
    capacity)
144 Port automatic leading edge slat
    (open)
145 Wing fences
146 Vortex generators
147 Aileron control rod linkage
148 Leading edge ribs
149 Wing centre spar
150 Main undercarriage hydraulic
    retraction jack
151 Undercarriage leg pivot
mounting
152 Slat guide rail fuel sealing can
153 Port mainwheel
154 Mainwheel door
155 Position of landing lamp on starboard
    mainwheel door
156 Approach lights
157 Retractable catapult hook
158 Cranked wing front spar
159 Aileron servo control
160 Mk 12 20 mm cannon
161 Spent cartridge case and link ejector
    chutes
162 Mainwheel well
163 Centre-line pylon (3575 lb/1622 kg)
    capacity
164 150 US gal (568 l) fuel tank
165 Inboard wing pylon (2240 lb/1016 kg)
    capacity
166 400 US gal (1514 l) long-range fuel
    tank
167 Snakeye 500 lb (227 kg) retarded
    bomb
168 Mk 83 1000 lb (454 kg) HE bomb

135 Tip fairing
136 Aileron horn balance
137 Wing tip antenna fairing
138 Port navigation light
139 LAU-10A Zuni rocket launcher
140 5-in (12.7-cm) folding fin rocket
141 AGM-12 Bullpup air-to-ground missile

# Vought A-7E Corsair II

1 Upward hingeing radome
2 Radar scanner dish
3 AN/APQ-126 radar equipment module
4 Scanner tracking mechanism
5 Radar mounting bulkhead
6 Dual pitot heads
7 Windscreen rain dispersal air ducts
8 Radar transmitter/receiver equipment
9 Cooling air exit louvres
10 Engine air intake
11 Forward radar warning antenna
12 Marker beacon aerial
13 Catapult launch bar
14 Intake duct framing
15 Cockpit floor level
16 Boron carbide (HCF) cockpit armour panelling
17 Cockpit pressurisation valve
18 Armoured front pressure bulkhead
19 Rudder pedals
20 Control column
21 Instrument panel
22 Head-down projected map display
23 Instrument panel shroud
24 Armoured windscreen panels
25 AN/ALQ-7[V] head-up-display [HUD]
26 Retractable flight refuel ling probe
27 Pilot's rear view mirrors
28 Cockpit canopy cover, upward hinged
29 Ejection seat headrest
30 Seat arming/safety lever
31 Safety harness
32 McDonnell Douglas Escapac 1-C2 rocket powered 'zero-zero' ejection seat
33 Starboard side console panel
34 External canopy 1atch
35 Engine throttle 1eve r
36 Port side console panel
37 Static ports
38 Kick-in boarding steps
39 Cannon muzzle aperture
40 Extending boarding ladder
41 Deck approach 1ights
42 Taxying lamp
43 Nose undercarriage leg strut
44 Levered suspension axle beam
45 Twin nosewheels, aft retracting
46 Nosewheel doors
47 Cannon barrels
48 Intake trunking
49 Cockpit rear pressure bulkhead
50 Incidence transmitter
51 Electrical system equipment bay
52 Ejection seat launch rails
53 Canopy aft framing
54 Hydraulic canopy jack
55 Canopy hinge point
56 TACAN aerial
57 Ammunition feed drive mechanism
58 Canopy emergency release
59 Ammunition feed and link return chutes
60 M61A1 Vulcan 20 mm rotary cannon
61 Gun gas spill duct

62 Rotary cannon/ammunition drive, flexible interconnection
63 Cannon bay, air conditioning pack on starboard side
64 Liquid oxygen converter
65 Emergency hydraulic accumulator
66 Electronics systems built-in test equipment (BITE) panel
67 Ground power socket
68 Ventral doppler navigation aerial
69 Port avionics equipment bay
70 Cooling air extractor fan
71 Forward fuselage fuel cell; total internal fuel capacity 1249 US gal (5678 l)
72 Fuselage stores pylon, capacity 500 lbs (227 kg)
73 Wing front spar/fuselage attachment pin joint
74 Control rod runs
75 Ammunition drum, 1000-rounds
76 UHF aerial
77 Centre-section integral fuel tank
78 Wing panel centre-section carry-through structure
79 Wing skin panel centreline joint strap
80 Upper anti-collision light
81 Starboard wing integral fuel tank
82 Fuel system piping
83 Pylon attachment hardpoints
84 Inboard leading edge flap, lowered

85 Flap hydraulic actuators
86 Centre wing pylon, capacity 3500 lbs (1558 kg)
87 AIM-9L Sidewinder air-to-air missile
88 Fuselage missile pylon
89 Missile launch rail
90 FLIR (forward-looking infra-red) pod carried on starboard inboard pylon
91 Mk 82 500 lb (227 kg) HE bombs
92 Tripple ejector rack (TER)
93 Leading-edge dog-tooth
94 Wing fold hydraulic jack
95 Outer wing panel hinge joint

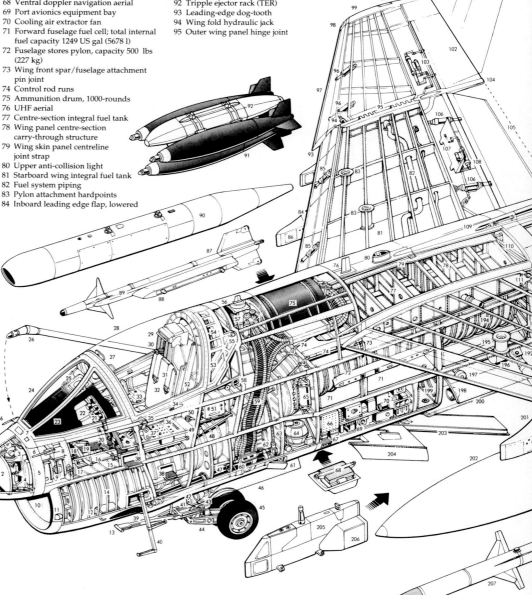

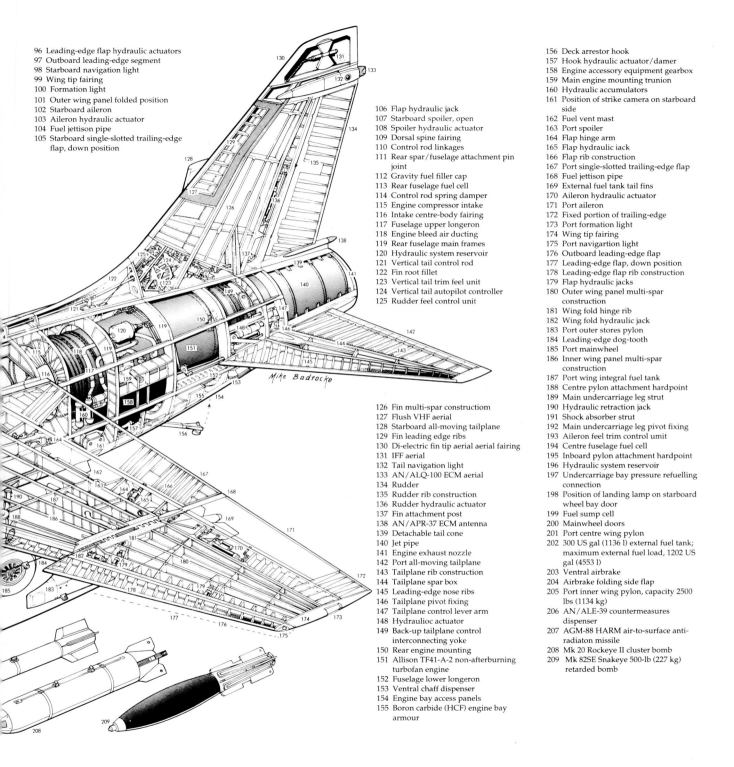

96 Leading-edge flap hydraulic actuators
97 Outboard leading-edge segment
98 Starboard navigation light
99 Wing tip fairing
100 Formation light
101 Outer wing panel folded position
102 Starboard aileron
103 Aileron hydraulic actuator
104 Fuel jettison pipe
105 Starboard single-slotted trailing-edge flap, down position

106 Flap hydraulic jack
107 Starboard spoiler, open
108 Spoiler hydraulic actuator
109 Dorsal spine fairing
110 Control rod linkages
111 Rear spar/fuselage attachment pin joint
112 Gravity fuel filler cap
113 Rear fuselage fuel cell
114 Control rod spring damper
115 Engine compressor intake
116 Intake centre-body fairing
117 Fuselage upper longeron
118 Engine bleed air ducting
119 Rear fuselage main frames
120 Hydraulic system reservoir
121 Vertical tail control rod
122 Fin root fillet
123 Vertical tail trim feel unit
124 Vertical tail autopilot controller
125 Rudder feel control unit

126 Fin multi-spar constructiom
127 Flush VHF aerial
128 Starboard all-moving tailplane
129 Fin leading edge ribs
130 Di-electric fin tip aerial aerial fairing
131 IFF aerial
132 Tail navigation light
133 AN/ALQ-100 ECM aerial
134 Rudder
135 Rudder rib construction
136 Rudder hydraulic actuator
137 Fin attachment post
138 AN/APR-37 ECM antenna
139 Detachable tail cone
140 Jet pipe
141 Engine exhaust nozzle
142 Port all-moving tailplane
143 Tailplane rib construction
144 Tailplane spar box
145 Leading-edge nose ribs
146 Tailplane pivot fixing
147 Tailplane control lever arm
148 Hydraulioc actuator
149 Back-up tailplane control interconnecting yoke
150 Rear engine mounting
151 Allison TF41-A-2 non-afterburning turbofan engine
152 Fuselage lower longeron
153 Ventral chaff dispenser
154 Engine bay access panels
155 Boron carbide (HCF) engine bay armour

156 Deck arrestor hook
157 Hook hydraulic actuator/damer
158 Engine accessory equipment gearbox
159 Main engine mounting trunion
160 Hydraulic accumulators
161 Position of strike camera on starboard side
162 Fuel vent mast
163 Port spoiler
164 Flap hinge arm
165 Flap hydraulic iack
166 Flap rib construction
167 Port single-slotted trailing-edge flap
168 Fuel jettison pipe
169 External fuel tank tail fins
170 Aileron hydraulic actuator
171 Port aileron
172 Fixed portion of trailing-edge
173 Port formation light
174 Wing tip fairing
175 Port navigartion light
176 Outboard leading-edge flap
177 Leading-edge flap, down position
178 Leading-edge flap rib construction
179 Flap hydraulic jacks
180 Outer wing panel multi-spar construction
181 Wing fold hinge rib
182 Wing fold hydraulic jack
183 Port outer stores pylon
184 Leading-edge dog-tooth
185 Port mainwheel
186 Inner wing panel multi-spar construction
187 Port wing integral fuel tank
188 Centre pylon attachment hardpoint
189 Main undercarriage leg strut
190 Hydraulic retraction jack
191 Shock absorber strut
192 Main undercarriage leg pivot fixing
193 Aileron feel trim control umit
194 Centre fuselage fuel cell
195 Inboard pylon attachment hardpoint
196 Hydraulic system reservoir
197 Undercarriage bay pressure refuelling connection
198 Position of landing lamp on starboard wheel bay door
199 Fuel sump cell
200 Mainwheel doors
201 Port centre wing pylon
202 300 US gal (1136 l) external fuel tank; maximum external fuel load, 1202 US gal (4553 l)
203 Ventral airbrake
204 Airbrake folding side flap
205 Port inner wing pylon, capacity 2500 lbs (1134 kg)
206 AN/ALE-39 countermeasures dispenser
207 AGM-88 HARM air-to-surface anti-radiaton missile
208 Mk 20 Rockeye II cluster bomb
209 Mk 82SE Snakeye 500-lb (227 kg) retarded bomb

Mike Badrocke

# McDonnell-Douglas F/A-18C Hornet

1 Glassfibre radome
2 Radome open position
3 Planar radar scanner
4 Scanner tracking mechanism
5 Radome hinge point
6 Cannon muzzle aperture
7 Gun gas venting air intakes
8 Flight refuelling probe, extended
9 Cannon barrels
10 Radar module withdrawal rails
11 AN/ALQ-165 transmitting antenna
12. Electro-luminescent formation lighting strip
13 Hughes AN/APG-65 multi-mode radar equipment module
14 AN/ALR-67 receiving antenna
15 Ventral AN/ALQ-165 transmitting antenna
16 Radar beacon antenna
17 Pitot head, port and starboard
18 Angle of attack transmitter
19 Ammunition drum, 570 rounds
20 Cannon and ammunition drum hydraulic drive motor
21 Cannon mounting
22 Refuelling probe actuator
23 Frameless windscreen panel
24 Instrument panel shroud
25 M61A1 20 mm six barrel rotary cannon
26 Ammunition feed chute
27 Night identification spotlight (CF-18A aircraft only)
28 Cannon bay access panel
29 Gun bay purging air vents
30 Nosewheel doors
31 Ground power socket
32 Nose undercarriage wheel bay
33 Wing root leading-edge extension
34 Front pressure bulkhead
35 Rudder pedals
36 Control column, quadriplex fly-by-wire control system
37 Kaiser multi-function CRT head-down displays
38 Kaiser AN/AVQ-28 head-up display
39 Upward hinged cockpit canopy
40 Pilot's rear view mirrors
41 Canopy open position
42 Ejection seat headrest
43 Starboard side console panel
44 Martin-Baker SJU-5/6 ejection seat
45 Engine throttle levers
46 Port side console panel
47 Cockpit floor level
48 Avionics equipment bay, port and starboard
49 Landing lamp
50 Catapult launch signal lights
51 Hydraulic steering control
52 Catapult launch strop
53 Twin nosewheels, forward retracting
54 Boarding ladder, extended
55 Hydraulic retraction jack
56 Cleveland nose undercarriage leg strut
57 UHF/TACAN aerial

58 Liquid oxygen converter
59 Cabin pressure regulator
60 Underfloor avionics equipment bay
61 Structural space provision for second seat (FA-18D)
62 Canopy actuator
63 Canopy lock actuator
64 Rear pressure bulkhead
65 Canopy hinge point
66 Rear avionics equipment bays, port and starboard
67 Fuselage centreline pylon
68 Leading-edge extension frame construction
69 Fuselage void fire suppression foam filler
70 Forward fuselage self-sealing bag-type fuel tanks; total internal capacity, 1415 Imp gal (1700 US gal/6435 l)
71 Fuselage top longeron
72 AN/ALQ-165 transmitting antennae
73 Starboard wing root leading-edge extension
74 Graphite/epoxy dorsal access panels
75 Starboard position light
76 Fin aerodynamic load alleviating strake
77 Intake ramp bleed air spill duct
78 TACAN aerial
79 Fuel tank access panels
80 Forward aircraft lifting fitting
81 Avionics equipment liquid cooling system heat exchanger
82 Air conditioning system ram air intake
83 Boundary layer splitter plate
84 Port position light
85 Intake ramp bleed air holes
86 Port engine intake
87 Intake duct framing
88 Cooling air spill ducts
89 Port load alleviating strake
90 Air conditioning plant
91 Boundary layer spill duct
92 Air conditioning heat exchanger exhaust
93 Leading-edge flap hydraulic motor and drive shaft

94 Wing root bolted attachment joints
95 Centre section self-sealing fuel tanks
96 Fuel bay deck
97 Engine bleed air duct to air conditioning system
98 UHF/IFF/Data Link antenna
99 Starboard wing root joint
100 Inboard stores pylon
101 Mk 82, 500-lb (227 kg) Snakeye retarded bombs
102 Multiple ejector rack
103 Outboard stores pylon
104 Starboard wing integral fuel tank
105 Wing fold joint
106 Leading-edge flap, down position
107 Flap rotary hinge actuator
108 Ventral navigation light panelling
109 Graphite/epoxy wing skin panelling
110 Starboard navigation light
111 Missile launch rail
112 AIM-9L Sidewinder air-to-air missile
113 Electro luminescent formation lights
114 Wing tip folded position
115 Starboard drooping aileron
116 Aileron hydraulic actuator
117 Wing fold hydraulic actuator
118 Flap vane

119 Port single-slotted flap, down position
120 Flap external hinge
121 Flap tandem hydraulic actuator
122 Rear fuselage self-sealing fuel tank
123 Hydraulic reservoirs, port and starboard

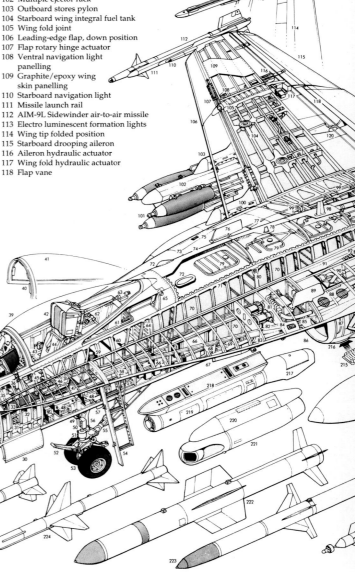

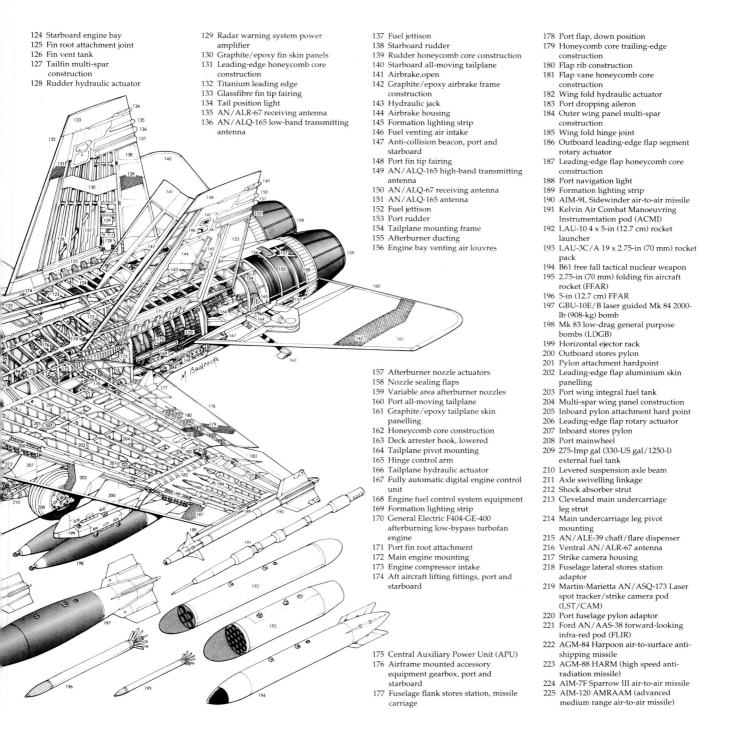

124 Starboard engine bay
125 Fin root attachment joint
126 Fin vent tank
127 Tailfin multi-spar construction
128 Rudder hydraulic actuator
129 Radar warning system power amplifier
130 Graphite/epoxy fin skin panels
131 Leading-edge honeycomb core construction
132 Titanium leading edge
133 Glassfibre fin tip fairing
134 Tail position light
135 AN/ALR-67 receiving antenna
136 AN/ALQ-165 low-band transmitting antenna
137 Fuel jettison
138 Starboard rudder
139 Rudder honeycomb core construction
140 Starboard all-moving tailplane
141 Airbrake, open
142 Graphite/epoxy airbrake frame construction
143 Hydraulic jack
144 Airbrake housing
145 Formation lighting strip
146 Fuel venting air intake
147 Anti-collision beacon, port and starboard
148 Port fin tip fairing
149 AN/ALQ-165 high-band transmitting antenna
150 AN/ALQ-67 receiving antenna
151 AN/ALQ-165 antenna
152 Fuel jettison
153 Port rudder
154 Tailplane mounting frame
155 Afterburner ducting
156 Engine bay venting air louvres
157 Afterburner nozzle actuators
158 Nozzle sealing flaps
159 Variable area afterburner nozzles
160 Port all-moving tailplane
161 Graphite/epoxy tailplane skin panelling
162 Honeycomb core construction
163 Deck arrester hook, lowered
164 Tailplane pivot mounting
165 Hinge control arm
166 Tailplane hydraulic actuator
167 Fully automatic digital engine control unit
168 Engine fuel control system equipment
169 Formation lighting strip
170 General Electric F404-GE-400 afterburning low-bypass turbofan engine
171 Port fin root attachment
172 Main engine mounting
173 Engine compressor intake
174 Aft aircraft lifting fittings, port and starboard
175 Central Auxiliary Power Unit (APU)
176 Airframe mounted accessory equipment gearbox, port and starboard
177 Fuselage flank stores station, missile carriage
178 Port flap, down position
179 Honeycomb core trailing-edge construction
180 Flap rib construction
181 Flap vane honeycomb core construction
182 Wing fold hydraulic actuator
183 Port dropping aileron
184 Outer wing panel multi-spar construction
185 Wing fold hinge joint
186 Outboard leading-edge flap segment rotary actuator
187 Leading-edge flap honeycomb core construction
188 Port navigation light
189 Formation lighting strip
190 AIM-9L Sidewinder air-to-air missile
191 Kelvin Air Combat Manoeuvring Instrumentation pod (ACMI)
192 LAU-10 4 x 5-in (12.7 cm) rocket launcher
193 LAU-3C/A 19 x 2.75-in (70 mm) rocket pack
194 B61 free fall tactical nuclear weapon
195 2.75-in (70 mm) folding fin aircraft rocket (FFAR)
196 5-in (12.7 cm) FFAR
197 GBU-10E/B laser guided Mk 84 2000-lb (908-kg) bomb
198 Mk 83 low-drag general purpose bombs (LDGB)
199 Horizontal ejector rack
200 Outboard stores pylon
201 Pylon attachment hardpoint
202 Leading-edge flap aluminium skin panelling
203 Port wing integral fuel tank
204 Multi-spar wing panel construction
205 Inboard pylon attachment hard point
206 Leading-edge flap rotary actuator
207 Inboard stores pylon
208 Port mainwheel
209 275-Imp gal (330-US gal/1250-l) external fuel tank
210 Levered suspension axle beam
211 Axle swivelling linkage
212 Shock absorber strut
213 Cleveland main undercarriage leg strut
214 Main undercarriage leg pivot mounting
215 AN/ALE-39 chaff/flare dispenser
216 Ventral AN/ALR-67 antenna
217 Strike camera housing
218 Fuselage lateral stores station adaptor
219 Martin-Marietta AN/ASQ-173 Laser spot tracker/strike camera pod (LST/CAM)
220 Port fuselage pylon adaptor
221 Ford AN/AAS-38 forward-looking infra-red pod (FLIR)
222 AGM-84 Harpoon air-to-surface anti-shipping missile
223 AGM-88 HARM (high speed anti-radiation missile)
224 AIM-7F Sparrow III air-to-air missile
225 AIM-120 AMRAAM (advanced medium range air-to-air missile)

# Specifications

## McDonnell Douglas A-4M

**Wing:** span 27 ft 6 in (8.38 m); area 260.0 sq ft (24.155m²)
**Fuselage and tail:** length excluding probe 40 ft 3.5 in (12.27 m); height 15 ft 0 in (4.57 m); tailplane span 11 ft 3.5 in (3.44 m)
**Powerplant:** one Pratt & Whitney J52-P-408 rated at 11,200 Ib (50.0 kN) dry thrust
Weights: empty 10,465 Ib (4747 kg); maximum take-off 24,500 Ib (11,113 kg)
**Fuel and load:** internal fuel 4434 Ibs (2011 kg); external fuel up to three 300-US gal (1136-litre) drop tanks; max ordnance 9155 Ibs (4153 kg)
**Speed:** maximum level speed 'clean' at 25,000 ft (7620 m) 625 mph (1006 km/h); maximum speed 'clean' at sea level 685 mph (1102 km/h)
**Range:** ferry range 2000 miles (3225 km); combat radius with a 4000-lb (1814-kg) warload 340 miles (547 km)
**Performance:** maximum rate of climb at sea level 10,300 ft (3140 m) per minute, service ceiling 38,700 ft (11,795 m); take-off run 2730 ft (832 m) at 23,000-lb (10,433-kg) weight

## McDonnell Douglas TA-4F

generally similar to the A-4M Skyhawk II except in the following details:
**Fuselage and tail:** length 42 ft 7.25 in (12.98 m); height 15 ft 3 in (4.65 m)
**Powerplant:** one Pratt & Whitney J52-P-8A rated at 9300 Ibs (41.3 kN) dry thrust
**Weights:** empty 10,602 Ibs (4809 kg), normal take-off 15,783 Ibs (7159 kg)
**Fuel and load:** internal fuel 660 US gal (2498 l)
**Speed:** maximum level speed 'clean' at sea level 675 mph (1086 km/h)
**Range:** ferry range 2200 miles (3540 km); normal range 1350 miles (2175 km)
**Performance:** maximum rate of climb at sea level 5750 ft (1753 m) per minute, take-off run 3380 ft (1030 m) at 23,000-lb (10,433-kg) weight

## McDonnell Douglas TA-4J

similar to the TA-4F Skyhawk except in the following details:
**Powerplant:** one Pratt & Whitney J52-P-6 rated at 8500 Ibs (37.7 kN) dry thrust

## Vought A-7E

**Wing:** span 38 ft 9 in (11.81 m); width folded 23 ft 9 in (7.24 m); aspect ratio 4.0; area 375.0 sq ft (34.83 m²)
**Fuselage and tail:** length 46 ft 1.5 in (14.06 m); height 16 ft 0 in (4.88 m); tailplane span 18 ft 1.5 in (5.52 m); wheel base 15 ft 10 in (4.83 m)
**Powerplant:** one Allison TF41-A-2 rated at 15,000 Ibs (66.6 kN) dry thrust

**Weights:** empty equipped 19,915 Ibs (8988 kg); normal take-off 29,000 Ibs (13,154 kg); maximum take off 42,000 Ib (19,050 kg)
**Fuel and load:** internal fuel 9263 Ibs (4202 kg); external fuel up to four 300-US gal (1136 litre) drop tanks; maximum ordnance 20,000 Ibs (9072 kg) nominal, about 15,000 Ib (6804 kg) practical with reduced internal fuel and 9500 Ibs (4309 kg) practical with maximum internal fuel
**Speed:** maximum level speed 'clean' at sea level 698 mph (1123 km/h)
**Range:** ferry range 2871 miles (4621 km) with external fuel or 2281 miles (3671 km) on internal fuel; combat radius 715 miles (1151 km) on a hi-lo-hi mission
**Performance:** maximum rate of climb at sea level 15,000 ft (4572 m) per minute; service ceiling 42,000 ft (12,800 m) take-off run 5000 ft (1524 m) at maximum take-off weight; take-off distance to 50 ft (15 m) 5865 ft (1790 m); landing distance from 50 ft (15 m) 4695 ft (1430 m)

## McDonnell Douglas AV-8B

**Wing:** span 30 ft 4 in (9.25 m); aspect ratio 4.0; area 338.7 sq ft (22.18 m²) including two 4.35-sq ft (0.40 m²) LERXs
**Fuselage and tail:** length 46 ft 4 in (14.12 m); height 11 ft 7.75 in (3.55 m); tailplane span 13 ft 11 in (4.24 m); wheel base 11 ft 4 in (3.45 m)
**Powerplant:** one Rolls-Royce F402-RR-406A rated at 21,450 Ibs (95.42 kN) dry thrust
**Weights:** operating empty 13,086 Ibs (5936 kg); normal take-off 22,950 Ibs (10,410 kg) for 9-g operation; maximum take-off 31,000 Ibs (14,061 kg) for 1330 ft (405 m) STO or 18,950 Ibs (8595 kg) for VTO
**Fuel and load:** internal fuel 7759 Ibs (3519 kg); external fuel up to 8070 Ibs (3661 kg) in four 300-US gal (1136-litre) drop tanks; maximum ordnance 9200 Ibs (4173 kg)
**Speed:** maximum level speed 'clean' at sea level 661 mph (1065 km/h)
**Range:** ferry range 2418 miles (3891 km) with empty tanks discarded or 2015 miles (3243 km) with empty tanks retained; combat radius 103 miles (167 km) with a one hour loiter after a 1200-ft (366-m) STO with 12 Mk 82 Snakeye bombs, or 553 miles (889 km) on a hi-lo-hi mission after a 1200-ft (366-m) STO with a 4000-lb (1814-kg) load, including seven Mk 82 Snakeye bombs, or 722 miles (1162 km) on a deck-launched interception mission with two AIM-9 Sidewinders and two drop tanks; combat air patrol radius, with a 3-hour patrol endurance, 115 miles (185 km)
**Performance:** maximum rate of climb at sea level 14,715 ft (4485 m) per minute; service ceiling more than 50,000 ft (15,240 m); STO distance 1330 ft (405 m) at maximum take-off weight

## McDonnell Douglas/British Aerospace TAV-8B

similar to the AV-8B except in the following details:
**Fuselage and tail:** length 50 ft 3 in (15.32 m)
**Weights:** operating empty 14,223 Ibs (6451 kg)

## McDonnell Douglas F/A-18C

**Wing:** span over missile rails 36 ft 6 in (11.43 m) and over wingtip missiles 40 ft 4.75 in (12.31 m); aspect ratio 3.5; area 400.0 sq ft (37.16 m²)
**Fuselage and tail:** length 56 ft 0 in (17.07 m); height 15 ft 3.5 in (4.66 m); tailplane span 21 ft 7.25 in (6.58 m); wheel base 17 ft 9.5 in (5.42 m)
**Powerplant:** two General Electric F404-GE-400 each rated at about 16,000 Ibs (71.2 kN) afterburning thrusts
**Weights:** empty 23,050 Ibs (10,455 kg); normal take-off 36,710 Ibs (16,652 kg) for a fighter mission; maximum take-off 49,224 Ibs (22,328 kg) for an attack mission
**Fuel and load:** internal fuel 10,860 Ibs (4926 kg); external fuel up to 6732 Ibs (3053 kg) in three 330-US gal (1250 litre) drop tanks; maximum ordnance 17,000 Ib (7711 kg)
**Speed:** maximum level speed 'clean' at high altitude more than 1190 mph (1915 km/h)
**Range:** ferry range with internal and external fuel more than 2303 miles (3706 km); combat radius more than 460 miles (740 km) on a fighter mission, or 662 miles (1065 km) on an attack mission
**Performance:** maximum rate of climb at sea level 45,000 ft (13,715 m) per minute; combat ceiling about 50,000 ft (15,240 m); take-off run less than 1400 ft (427 m)

## McDonnell Douglas F/A-18A

generally similar to the F/A-18C except in the following particulars:
**Weights:** normal take-off 33,585 Ib (15,234 kg) for a fighter mission; maximum take-off 48,253 Ib (21,888 kg) for an attack mission

## McDonnell Douglas F/A-18B

generally similar to the F/A-18A except in the following details:
**Weights:** normal take-off 33,585 Ibs (15,234 kg) for a fighter mission; maximum take-off 47,000 Ibs (21,319 kg) for an attack mission
**Fuel and load:** internal fuel reduced by less than six per cent to provide volume for the accommodation of the second seat
**Range:** ferry range with internal and external fuel 2187 miles (3520 km); combat radius 634 miles (1020 km) on an attack mission